The Mad Habit

by M Sarki

Also by M Sarki:

Zimble Zamble Zumble (limited edition, elimae books 2000) poetry

Zimble Zamble Zumble (trade edition, Author's Choice Press 2002) poetry

Little War Machine (Ravenna Press 2004) poetry

Mewl House (Rogue Literary Society 2005) poetry

Any Fucking Day (Rogue Literary Society 2009) poetry

Diary of the Modern God (Rogue Literary Society 2009)

Photographs: People, Places, and Nudes (Rogue Literary Society 2009)

Triple No. 2: No Entry (Ravenna Press 2012) poetry

Shorter Prose (Rogue Literary Society 2013)

Stamped Against the Night (Rogue Literary Society 2014)

Material to Destroy (Rogue Literary Society 2014)

No Entry (Rogue Literary Society 2014) poetry

Ailene Nou (Rogue Literary Society 2017)

...When all the days were mine.___M Sarki

COPYRIGHT

DEDICATION

For Beverly Lane and Gordon Lish

Table of Contents

...Often far away there I thought of these two, guarding the door of Darkness, knitting black wool as for a warm pall, one introducing, introducing continuously to the unknown, the other scrutinizing the cheery and foolish faces with unconcerned old eyes. Ave! Old knitter of black wool. Morituri te salutant. Not many of those she looked at ever saw her again—not half, by a long way. ___from *Heart of Darkness*, Part 1 by Joseph Conrad

... The details must be told only through a veil of oblivion which is itself a medium of memory, for there is no forgetfulness even of the smallest thing. If it is hidden, it is revealed through its absence, the sense of the void. ___from *Miss MacIntosh, My Darling* by Marguerite Young

Foreword

Not long ago my wife dubiously asked me twice if I really liked the new shower curtain and bath towels because, she remarked, when her twin sister was visiting us she never said a word about whether she liked them, or not. I asked my spouse to please stop worrying about what other people think, and consider never expecting confirmation or excitement about anything you might produce artistically as few, if any people, really care. Later that same afternoon I revised my rather blunt statement. I kindly then expressed how important it is that her art not be mediated. I counseled her that creating something with the outright interest of pleasing somebody else is a recipe for disaster. I added that one must continue to evolve and be surrounded by those things which satisfy and impel us to continually bring forth. Eventually, I went on to say, a day will come when a friend or acquaintance will actually remark how lovely our bathroom creation and entire home truly is. I further said that the sincerity of a remark such as this will then be obvious to her, and for that one brief instant she might then indulge herself in a moment of sanctity. But I added that any wallowing of hers best be as fleeting as the rare instant in which comments such as these are made. These instructions I made to her regarding mediated art also have everything to do as well with this, my own writing project, now spanning three years and counting. And of course I fear I am delusional and have gone too far to now do anything about it. My inner war is constant. The internal shaming and belittling messages never stop, and feelings of inadequacy and guilt haunt me daily.

The accounting that follows places itself within a specific time frame spanning the years 1995 through 2017. And I believe in my heart that one of these main characters, my teacher, editor, and friend Gordon Lish will be remembered for what he gave the literary world through his tyrannical teaching, editing, and authoring of his own work. I am impelled to give an accounting of our relationship in order to counteract anything that might be reported by another critic not so flattering nor tolerant of our relationship. In his teaching, Gordon insisted that a writer maintain a required gaze upon the object. When writing short poems I learned it was paramount to do so, and by default, I found it much easier to compose verse in this manner. But when faced with crafting a longer work, and one that encourages digression in many forms, the task itself becomes at times overwhelming and insurmountable. Life does not behave in a non-digressive manner so why does writing have to? Untold events alter everything.

But often, I realize, truth escapes us in lieu of embellishment. Disappointments exceed expectations. Rarely will our own lens remain crystal clear, and the dust that clouds our view often has more to do with how and what we feel instead of what actually happened. In *Winter Notes on Summer Impressions,* Fyodor Dostoevsky wrote that his readers do not require accuracy but rather his *personal but sincere observations*. I am keen to the nuances of every affair examined concerning my life, especially in regards to matters relating to my heart. But it is my ensuing bouts with despair that tend to immobilize me, freezing my fantasies, and creating chaotic emotions caused by fear. I am at a loss to explain my actions otherwise.

Today's social media platform provides ample opportunity in which a person might air out his laundry. I refuse those mediums. It is hoped that whatever follows on these pages simply exists as *scattered crumbs* that depict within a somewhat surprisingly elaborate and verbose critical book review such things as an adulterous failure, my own disastrous fall from a cabin roof, and a purely crappy event in which my wife tumbles head over heels onto the concrete walk outside our apartment in order to save our new puppy. And classically, the only instruments allowed in such a geometric construction as this would prove to be a compass and straightedge. Still, a labyrinth must be navigated properly, and for this artist, as Gordon Lish would say, *a difficulty must be overcome*. Actually, what shall proceed is more in the realm of a storied love affair. And a poet being made in spite of it all. And a teacher, of course, who emerges to guide them. A deep friendship and gratitude therefore begs for an expression beyond a simple thank you. An architecture thus emerges in which a sexual triangle is born.

But a fateful impairment devolves and then

disagreeably blocks the conduction of this fated adultery. It did give our impediment its rise, especially after having sustained itself for so many years, and at times given to fitful degrees, a collaboration that developed into a wondrous seduction. And to finally have all three of us arrive at the threshold of our sexual fantasy, our triangle present and attending itself to this ill-formed but perfect illusion, was nothing less than breathtaking. The expected outcome factored by persistent whispers of its delectable presumptions, in ways already secretly agreed upon. But as cowards do, we fled.

There are far too many contradictions in which to reconcile an actual life lived to the one potentially forecast. Environment is detrimental to the development of any life worth living. Both my wife and I were raised by strict Lutheran parents aspiring to higher social rankings than their own individual characters and cultural environment might have allowed for. As such, certain pressures were naturally exerted on their children. For example, strict orders to behave in manners as if evolved from a higher social ranking than they themselves came from. But I was never the smartest, the most handsome, most athletic, the toughest, wildest, bravest of all the other boys I grew up with. I was average, perhaps a bit above, but simply good at almost everything I put my hand to. The books I read and the music I listened to did allow for considering myself more interesting than the typical boring boys skipping stones and whistling all around me. But I always felt myself woefully different, and could never quite fit inside a group that I hadn't already established myself as leader. I struggled with this feeling for years. And finally, at the age of thirty-two, within the throes of a purely exasperating addiction to alcohol, I finally accepted my particular *difference* and, as Aristotle once advised, began to stand on it as does a genius. I also found it reliable to learn that wizardry, too often, involves itself in pointless pursuits.

Chapter 1: A Flower's Heart

My 2013 summer writing project, the year prior to the genesis of this one, consisted of composing a longer work titled *Stamped Against the Night*, and in the afterword I detailed the process involved in writing the book. Gordon Lish has never commented on anything regarding this previous work and he had no involvement in it in any capacity. I simply mailed him a signed copy and dedicated the book to him. He may have disapproved of the publication of *Stamped Against the Night* but he has never said to me personally or publicly anything good or bad regarding it. I suggest this will be the case from here on out. Early in 2017 I finally suspended my allegiance for including the great Lish in all my dedications when the Rogue Literary Society published my salacious fiction titled *Ailene Nou*, and Gordon will now likely forget one day, as he has done to others, that I ever existed. But we do have a history together. I maintain an extensive library of his own fiction elaborately signed and inscribed to me on page after page as well as an enormous collection of correspondence between the two of us. Early in our relationship I used to be intimidated by him, but that was many years ago. Tragically falling off a roof as I have done, does have its advantages in regards to individually understanding our ultimate insignificance and certain-to-come mortality. But I still have enormous love and respect for Gordon Lish. And my gratitude for what he did for me remains colossal.

There should never be the first thought which might harbor, for even a moment within these pages, that I am to set about attempting to raise the stature of Gordon Lish, or even to the contrary, presume me cutting the great man down to size. If the latter were actually so I myself might shrink away in shame enough to frightfully disappear. And if I were to attempt to glorify the teacher more than others already have, or will in the coming days and years, the idea again would be nothing short of preposterous. But what is more important to note, in the impending construction of this accounting, would be the finer points of our relationship, the friendly connection that was unique from his many other associations. The lettered man knew, certainly in the course of his long life, many people, their numbers countless perhaps. But it is my aim to present another side of Gordon Lish, and one that many others, besides myself, were also privy to in different ways. I might contend that individuals who may have known Lish best also shared the same bed with him. And of those, most likely, a figure that amounts to more than a few.

I began my latest project with a goal in mind that by re-reading the book *Sunshine* I would somehow come to my own resolution regarding the personal and professional relationship between Gordon and myself. The title also seemed to connect everything Gordon and I had ever been through, and the book's continued haunting of me from its resting place on my shelf continued its, at times, incessant harassment. It seems ironic, now that I have finished reading *Sunshine* again, that there never was a resolution, at least, in that book. And it is possible that resolutions, in the end, tend to generally remain in hiding just as the main character Freddy did.

Chapter 2: There Was No Boat Which Would Not Leak

My earliest intimacy with Gordon Lish may have been initiated sometime in the mid-nineties with my first reading of *Sunshine*. Clifford Hagen supposedly wrote this slim volume published by Harper & Row back in 1971, but I had my reasons for thinking Gordon Lish may have written it instead. I had been reading and writing back and forth to my newest obsession since sometime in 1987 as I had basically traded my chronic alcohol abuse for a literary relationship with Gordon Lish. And I was hell-bent to find out what I called *the truth* about everything I could. I knew Lish, by his own admission, had been involved in many ghost-writing activities for quite some time but he had, for the most part, kept them secret from the curious public. I was thinking, with my discovery of *Sunshine*, that I may have discovered one of them on my own.

Of the many books Lish has been instrumental in creating under assumed or other names, the most well-known and sophisticated is the longish autobiographical title *Coming Out of the Ice* by Victor Herman. On the dedication page Mr. Herman mentions those to whom he owes in the production of this book and among them was a person *"whose connection with this book is absolute, but because he asks that his name not be cited, I will enter the initials of his son, A.A.L., and state the wish of the father that the boy one day read herein, to know the heart of a man."* That son was none other than Atticus Augustus

Lish, the last and only son of the union between Gordon and his late wife Barbara. *Coming Out of the Ice* was published in 1979 and it is without a doubt the makings of a man other than Victor Herman with the presence of obvious nuances that could only have been produced by Gordon Lish. The Lilly Library in Bloomington, Indiana has the audio tapes of the hours of interviews between Lish and Herman which established the basis for what Lish was to eventually write to certain acclaim by notable critics such as William F. Buckley. Lish wrote many books that conceal his name as author, but further enquiry is appropriate to any literary investigator impelled to get to the bottom of things such as I am wont to do. I admit to not being privy to the entire list of these ghost-written or pseudo books, but I have collected copies of quite a few of them, and Gordon more than once informed me there were many more besides. Writing these books is how he made his small fortune, but it seems he is a bit ashamed of them, enough that he is not quite comfortable in revealing the list in total. Jim Garrison's book, *The Star Spangled Contract* being another title Lish had decided to be forthcoming with to me. Lish's voice is predominant in most everything he writes. It is something he cannot help, and I am given to doubt that he really wants to make it ever less so.

There is a monstrously physical element in the mystery behind the goings of Gordon Lish. Often it is obvious when talking to him face to face or on the telephone that he is *trying stories out*, seeing which ones fit, and what lies of his own to call truths and what truths he might call his fiction. However, any occasion in the past in which I believed he was telling me an untruth turned out to be not so, and there were enough of these instances that I eventually gave up my incessant need to know what exactly. I finally accepted all of what he had to say as simply another one of his many compositions, or what would eventually become a fiction found inside a book. It was then I learned of my own need for relating a fictional life and for actually living one within the confines of my mind rather than my need to continually climb out on lofty tree limbs and break bones that never heal properly from beginning to end.

Chapter 3: Queen of the Foreplay Dissolve

Gordon Lish is an anomaly and that is why I was so attracted to him. His written responses to me in the early years of our literary relationship were in a sense cryptic until I finally was invited by him to participate in one of his infamous fiction-writing classes.

There was no way at the time that my family
could afford my attending one of these infamous
classes being held eighty miles away from where
we lived in Louisville. But my wife insisted I go,
and because of her I am beholden to both Gordon
Lish and Beverly Lane, and have until just
recently included both their names in every
dedication I have made on the pages of my books.
My understanding of his messages to me were
better understood the more I studied
fiction-writing under him. These classes lasted as
long as four days and required attendance of up to
ten hours each day in a classroom where he spoke
nonstop and never, ever, took a break. I recorded

extensive notes in every class I attended, and these notes have helped to mould me into the person and writer I have become. He made me, same as he created his fictions. But contrary to the opinions of his detractors, he insisted I live my life for me and nobody else. Without him I would be nothing as a writer, and I owe him much more than allegiance, I owe him my life. And for over twenty years I have held steadfast in my allegiance, defending him from unfair criticism, and always wanting to find a deeper and more permanent way into his life. Because of his advancing age Father Time says I have already had my allotted appointments with him. What is left of life for Gordon Lish remains for him alone. It is paramount now for me to step away in order to see what I might see and to make of myself something I might admire in another. But in order to do so favorably I think it best to rediscover how I got to this point by beginning as near to this coming into my own in my understanding of the man who got me here. And it began with *Sunshine,* and for me it is the best place in which to begin this journey.

Chapter 4: An Edifice of Faded Magnificence

Anyone who is a serious, working author, wants to sit down and write the one book that turns out to be the end-all to everything ever written in the history of literature. The one piece of literature that nobody ever forgets after reading it. Something you could not possibly make any better no matter how hard you tried or who was helping you. There haven't been many of these books written through the years. *To Kill a Mockingbird* is one of these I feel worthy of mention. The one-book wonder. A book that was so good and important in its time that Harper Lee felt no need to try to better it, and she certainly was not going to put out something less worthy to follow. That certainly is a most fatal mistake, and it is surprising how much trash is put out everyday and still they call it literature. Of course, Ms. Lee claims she had no designs on becoming famous for writing the great American novel, though some do suggest she did and should have gone on to write even more of them for posterity. And through the years, in the midst of my revising this manuscript, the national news reported that Harper Lee published in the spring of 2015 the book she wrote first which is actually a sequel to her masterpiece. There is some suspicion as to her mental state for agreeing to this publication of a work she maintained for many years she has never wanted published in her lifetime. And I have no interest in reading it.

All the biographical facts I have ever learned regarding the life of author Clifford Hagen I gathered from his book *Sunshine*. It isn't that I have not looked elsewhere and attempted to plumb deeper into his biography. I have. It states on the back of the dust jacket that Hagen was supposedly a southern writer born in 1941 and as far as I have been able to ascertain he simply fell off the face of the earth after publishing this little novel. There are no other books crediting Clifford Hagen as author. Looking back, my suspicious reasoning afforded me factors enough to suspect the name Clifford Hagen as a pseudonym for Gordon Lish. I became even more dubious as Hagen's picture was also on the back of the dust jacket and he strikingly resembled a younger Lish. There was a vibrancy present in his photograph, a wildness I guess that allowed my imagination to fire. I thought the photograph was of Lish and especially after I read the book I was convinced enough to even ask Gordon himself. In the meantime I read the book diligently, perhaps a bit like a detective, and I hadn't revisited the text again until I began this project in the summer of 2014. It was then that I brought the book back down from the shelf to take another look. I decided I would write an elaborate review of the book as I read it again. It is uncanny but the very best books implore me to write about them as I read them, taking notes, transcribing texts as quotes I must preserve if not for me than the person who might happen to eventually read what I might have had to say. But there is no plan for where my present exercise will take me, and whether or not anyone but myself will be interested in the project. At the very least my reading of *Sunshine* again will yield additional opportunities to reconsider my relationship with Gordon Lish and to learn something about myself in the process. Always I am wary of delusional thinking, and it is hoped the following text will reveal one or two thoughts I might have had back then, and whether or not my love for Gordon had been simply a lie or a fiction of my own making. For the sake of my own self worth I am hopeful of a result more redemptive than accusatory, and less erotic than my previous arousals indicated. But Gordon passionately taught in his classes, to men and to women both, to *write first with your dick* and then revise the results *with your mind*.

Chapter 5: Swinging on Broken Hinges

Yesterday I read a short chapter from a book by

the now-deceased Christopher Hitchens titled *Letters to a Young Contrarian* in which he mentored in a letter to a student to write *"as if"*. Hitchens gave several examples of dead writers who conducted their craft well while living in oppressed countries where it was illegal to publish work that the government did not first approve of. These particular writers mentioned by Hitchens all wrote *as if* no State laws were ever broken and they were actually free to say whatever it was they were impelled to produce on the page. Just as important as not being mediated in one's writing it is imperative that our truth reject the herd mentality, and a work that would turn popular to the masses is to be avoided at all costs. Hitchens emphasized the importance of not lying or showing cowardice. Of course, Hitchens was mainly speaking about being a contrarian in societies that disapproved of argument and healthy discourse in debate. It could be supposed he was speaking more about politics and social injustices, wars, famines, and a need to believe in something greater than ourselves. And to avoid at all costs an acquiescence to a leader who might guide us to this promised, but false, environment. But I believe Hitchens presented these words for me to also use as I see fit. And I am given to the proposition that we must talk about things that unsettle us. And I qualify that my accounting to follow here may not be at all what anyone else remembers who was actually present at the exact same time as these events progressed. Actual facts may be always blurred somewhat in literature, but that does not lessen the importance of the dialogue. Though threatened daily with thoughts of potential disapproval of me by others, and what I have chosen to retain on the page as memory, it is imperative I pursue this no matter the consequences.

For years I studied and wrote under the auspices of Gordon Lish. Much has been written about his teaching and editing practices and I imagine several examples of exposé will follow soon after he dies. He is eighty-three today at this date of publishing. As I have claimed numerous times in other articles and books already published that without the gifted Gordon Lish I would have become nothing of a writer. I sincerely believe that no matter how hard I had tried and applied myself I would never have written anything worth publishing. It was Gordon who freed me enough to become myself, to find my voice and the courage to express a certain truth demanded of my heart that would undoubtedly result in some form of jeopardy created on the page. I have produced four books of poetry edited by the hand of Gordon Lish. It was only on the publication of the fourth book of poems that I resisted the perpetual need to involve Gordon Lish as author of a foreword to that book. Instead, I wrote it myself in order to explain a comeback of sorts I would be making after having suffered a great injury due to a dreadful fall off the roof of my cabin in northern Michigan in 2010. It was because of this awful accident that I changed course in my life and decided to go on alone in my writing and publishing.

I did compose several poems after that dreadful day, and Gordon did continue to edit and approve them for publication. But soon enough the desire to compose poems quit coming for me and I felt a need to change the direction of my writing. Critical book reviews were resulting more from my hand, and I revisited the longer form of creative writing that some schools call prose. Gordon never sanctioned the new direction I was taking, but he also never outrightly discouraged me. Shortly after the fall from my roof I decided to make a few short art films which I created basically for myself. I felt fortunate that Gordon liked all of them very much and encouraged me to make more. But this desire to make films also soon faded as did the still amateur photography work that I had delved into around 1995 and basically had not done a lick of since the beginning of 2012.

Chapter 6: The White Skull Moon

Gordon Lish wrote a story he titled *The Death of Me* in which he relates his experience as a child on the last day of summer camp when all the kids would be competing in games, and medals would be awarded to all those day campers who performed their very best and at least placed in their specific competitions. He begins the story with the opening line, *I wanted to be amazing.* Not only was the story a brilliant example of writing, the entire piece spoke to me and my own desires even as an adult to one day be a famous writer. Early on, before studying under Gordon Lish, the genre of writing I wanted to be known for mattered little to me, only my own need to be famous for it. And of course, this is without a doubt the wrong reason for writing. One writes because one is a writer, not for fame nor fortune nor attention at all, but simply to write because one has no other choice but to. But I did not get to that purer idea until much later in my development. In fact, for some time Gordon held out little hope that I would ever become a writer of any note, and I suppose it was because he saw in me my selfish and grandiose need to be famous more than my necessary obsession to write. But I never quit, and I kept on writing and trying out new voices until I finally found my own, and then it became apparent to me that this was really all that mattered. To find one's own voice. And that is what I do these days. I write *as if* I am already respected and well-known. Fact is I do not need the money that comes with being famous, nor the attention writers seem to crave so much it often kills them.

ALFRED A. KNOPF

GORDON LISH

Mike —
Save yourself!
This ain't
how.

Chapter 7: In the Back of Beyond

Central Park in New York City is situated only a half block west of the home of Gordon Lish. And I never fail to feel his presence when I am in the vicinity. I know in my heart there was never a doubt that I was destined to be involved with Gordon Lish, same as he was with me, and as a result of this fated consequence, we also became friends. Several years ago, back in the late-nineties, on one of my family's annual fall visits to the city of New York, I strolled alone along the meandering paths of Central Park and eventually decided to rest my back in Harlem Meer on one of the long benches flanking the bronze sculpture of Hans Christian Andersen. This handsome gleaming statue features the famous author sitting and reading to a wayward duck. The actual man-made lake off to the side of this sculpture at Harlem Meer used to be a popular catch-and-release fishing destination that in summer was also used for swimming. On this particular early morning the lake was calm. I was flat on my back on the bench with eyes closed daydreaming, allowing my imagination to wander and hoping to compose a poem. It is my nature to use quiet moments to reflect back inside to a life that seems at once happening to me, though often it is I who erroneously believes to be the one in charge of it. I realized long ago that life is simply what I do and then what happens next. If possible, I strive for only what interests me, and as far as life in general goes, I only do what must be done. But I admit freely that there have been a few instances when I have pursued an event not likely to be in my best interest. But this particular day was not one of them.

Chapter 8: The Skin and Stalks of Grapes

April 30, 1988

Dear Mr. Lish,

Thank you for your interest in me! I have little time to write now, in this season of construction activity, and I have a rather large family to feed. I am determined to be a successful writer and will continue to work as time allows. I didn't realize there was so much to learn and by nature I am very impatient — when I get frustrated...

I respect the trade. I will earn my right to be published. I will accept guidance and criticism.

Is there a grant I may earn?

Is there a faster way out of construction and into writing for a living? — get this idea out of your head.

I am thrilled at your interest in me, and I promise I will continue to work on learning the skills necessary to speak honestly on the page.

Sincerely,
Michael T Seidl

Expanding literary concerns will one day certainly prove to be quite extensive concerning the life of Gordon Jay Lish. The many novels he published, his collections of short stories, his contributions to Jewish literary pursuits and periodicals, the occasional lawsuit entered into and against what he believed to be unethical publishing, his seventeen-year tenure as an editor at Knopf, a teaching career spanning over thirty years and held in private homes, his teaching fee financed by exorbitant tuitions afforded in general by only the most well-to-do and favored members of New York society. For many years Lish cut a dashing figure on the streets and corridors of this great city. There will be countless anecdotes published regarding his tyrannical editing and teaching practices. Already much has been made of his relationship with the gifted writer Raymond Carver whom Lish fiercely edited and of which, because of it, created such a magnificent literary buzz and new famous name.

The many facets and personalities of this Gordon Lish will also eventually be known throughout the varied landscape of untold remembrances to come, details meant to ignite one's appetite and suggest there was more involved in knowing the man than what was by design and made apparent by him. I contend that Lish controls his own media. But the hidden life of Gordon Lish will also one day reveal itself, and most likely, if truth be told, could actually have been the better part of his master plan. In years to come certain presentations will develop and clearly show that the moves Lish made on his board game of life were always calculated, and often he manipulated results to his advantage. I would not be surprised that anything written here and on the following pages, in essence, could be the covert result of Lish's own doing. It is possible that many, if not all, of these related individual personal experiences regarding Lish are being performed on his very own fiddle. There is rarely a moment when Gordon Lish is not creating something and generally crafting a *thing* for his eventual advantage.

Chapter 9: Blowing on the Coals

It is important to me, you could say it is an obsession, to follow every idea I have toward its conclusion no matter how ridiculous or unrealistic it might seem until it is abandoned or a meaningful end results. If there is to be an ending it must entail a version I can live with. My wife, stepson, and youngest son enjoy making fun of my bad ideas. And I deserve it. The honor and respect I have for my creative ideas insist that I follow them out to conclusions that at times go too far. There are occasions I am not careful enough about the consequences. But nothing has occurred yet that has caused me, or my family, any permanent damage. One of the favorite bad ideas my wife enjoys sharing for a laugh is the year I decided to go into the moped business. We lived at that time near Louisville in a little village outside of the city. It was a paradise cut out of expanding urban disease. For decades the wealthy had protected this area, and land prices kept the undesirables away. It was called a "tree city" and no limb could be touched without a review and permit issued by the organized, and official, tree police. It felt like a vacation seven days a week while living there. It was a good place to hide from work. We lived across from the village fire department in a little cape cod clad in solid, full one-inch redwood, clapboard. It was a house meant to stay active and alive. A few of the rugged firemen across the street drove Harley Davidson motorcycles, and though I hated speed and danger, I thought having a cool, two-wheel motorized bike would be not only fun, but a statement. I love easy recreation, lounging around and vegetating, and cruising about on a quiet motorized bike seemed pleasing to me. Nobody in Louisville was yet selling these mopeds, at least not any that looked classic or made sense to me. Online I found a company in Columbus, Ohio that sold an Indian-made bike called a Panther which seemed perfect for my plans. I decided I would drive the three hours up there, take a look at them, buy one outright and haul it home, and if I liked the bike enough I would go into business selling them. One of the first things I did when arriving home with my new contraption was spin over across the street on it and ask the Harley firemen if they thought I was a sissy? It was funny, and fun, being so obviously comfortable with my manhood. When I later rode over to a friend's home about five miles from me, he immediately wanted one of his own. I told him I needed to spend more time with mine and decide if the machine was actually reliable, if it would last, and how much maintenance and adjustments would be required to keep it on the road. But soon my confidence began to wane as adjustments constantly were required to keep the piece of shit running properly. The bike became for me another disappointment. What began as a social statement issuing from my personality turned into a sign of weakness. My kids got decent use out of the crappy machine, but I never felt good about my purchase ever again. But what made the story interesting for my wife and kids to tell was my carting her and the youngest one all the way to Columbus in the first place, hauling that thing home wedged upright in my company-owned van with my son having to ride for three and a half hours holding on to the heavy thing to keep it from falling over. It was a waste of both time and money, and not the first business venture I ever dreamed up that failed. What followed after that fiasco, because of my extensive experience in construction, I decided to buy a home correspondence course in order to earn a degree in the home inspection business. I seriously studied the curriculum and aced every test throughout the entire class, less the very last one. I never read the last chapter, nor did I take the final test that would have permitted me to become my own official home inspector and conduct business from my home. But I decided the work would be too boring for me. And just as I had years ago dreamed as a young paperboy of becoming a donut and bread maker, of wearing a tall, white baker's hat, I threw my books away. I seem to discard ideas as I do my friends, and that is why I have had so many and kept as few.

Chapter 10: Many Who Come for Wool Return Home Clipped and Shorn

One morning not so long ago, perhaps a week at best, I was reading a novella titled *Walking* by Thomas Bernhard and one of his characters by the name of Oehler was holding court with his companion about memory when he said,

...looking in the immediate proximity reveals nothing but incompetence. One should, in every case, go back over everything, even if it is in the depths of the past and scarcely ascertainable and discernible any longer. And that is what I suppose I am trying to do now when I look at what it is I have already written. But my *everything* is certainly not up to snuff with the work of others I have read. I just don't think the entirety of life is all that interesting. For the most part these memories I hear of bore me. I love the writings of Thomas Bernhard. Rancor is a word most likely used to describe him. He was definitely a disgruntled Austrian. It is because of him that I have been introduced to many other writers of note. Among them include the Swiss writer Robert Walser and, of course, the great German writer W.G. Sebald who liked to be called just Max. Max, like Bernhard, was none too happy over the state of his beloved homeland. But the common thread between these three men was their love for walking, for meandering about, traipsing across the countryside.

Some time ago I read a book by Sergio Chejfec titled *My Two Worlds* as it was suggested to me that I might like it seeing as though I loved books having to do with walking. And that is true, I do. There are so many great books written that have something or other to do with walking. Samuel Beckett's characters seem to do a bit of walking as do the roaming characters found in the writings of Thomas Bernhard, Robert Walser, and W. G. Sebald. And I like the characters in these books and want to know what, and how, they think. But

in Chejfec's *My Two Worlds* I did not much like
Sergio or his narrator. He, or they, had no
personality, or if they did it was a personality of
the pretentious type I do not like. The character
Sergio in *My Two Worlds* never felt as if he
belonged anywhere. He was always an outsider.
And the gulf existing between us is
insurmountable because, in contrast, I always feel
as if I belong. My problem is generally with the
people, not with where I am. I own this general
space surrounding me that enables free movement
wherever I am. I simply believe I occupy a holy
pocket and nobody has a right to violate it unless
he or she is invited and permitted to share in
communion with me. And I believe everybody
has this same holy swath so it isn't something
unique to myself that profits me or anoints me as
special. My youngest son would tell you I am
crazy, and that is all you need to know. He would
provide details regarding our trip to Paris where I
insisted to my family that the Parisians loved me
when in fact, according to my son, it was obvious
they hated me and made motions and faces
behind my back illustrating their distaste for
another disgusting American. In my own defense
I should tell you my son harbored perhaps a bit of
resentment as I held in our home a self-taught
required French-speaking class one night a week
for several weeks until our trip commenced, at
which time we were all on our own to speak this
foreign language any way we found possible. I
was of the opinion that I was doing quite well
with the limited French I did remember, and
believed it an honest attempt to at least speak the
language used in the country I was visiting. For

this I felt I deserved a free pass for my obvious failures to communicate, and even the occasional loving pat on the back would have seemed appropriate given the degree of my concerted efforts. But my son did not see it that way. He perceived me as being delusional about the Parisians sincere love for me. But again, this is a matter of that holy pocket that is sacred to me and something I am obviously willing to die for. But Sergio was not. He did not have this holy place surrounding him wherever he would go. This feeling of belonging was contrary to Chejfec. And for that reason alone I could not connect with him in his book nor listen to anything he had to say about water and birds and fish and how they all would stare at him. Granted, there was a period in my past when I did share those same feelings of not belonging, of being stared at, of feeling self-conscious that it was I who had done something wrong or was not good enough to be in the presence of these great people who were obviously better than me, or better at doing something in particular than I was, or maybe cooler, or their ancestry of better stock than mine. That is true, I did feel that way once, as do others at times feel the very same inadequacies that many of us go to therapy in order to work through, or else, eventually, simply off themselves by the obscene use of alcohol, drugs, guns, hanging, or even, if dreadfully serious, weighing oneself down enough to effect a complete drowning.

THE AMERICAN NATIONAL RED CROSS

This certifies that

Mike Sarki

is qualified as an

ADVANCED BEGINNER IN SWIMMING
having passed the required tests at

East Tawas

8/28/62

Alfred W. Cruttell
National Director
Safety Services

Chapter 11: The Cold Shift of Your Own Shadow

A few days ago I read a wonderful new collection of stories titled *Pond* written by Claire-Louise Bennett, a young British writer I recently discovered. What struck me even before I had completed what I eventually considered to be mis-categorized and instead actually a novel, my still having more than just a few pages remaining of the second to last piece, and still ahead of me a two page story to read before I could categorically say I was finished with this book, I already decided I was going to start right back in and read it all again. It is the rare book that challenges me so. I can only recall Robert Walser's *The Robber* having a similar effect, but that was because I had failed to understand his work enough, even though I loved it and thought *The Robber* certainly a masterpiece, but felt in order to do it justice I needed to get right back on it while it remained still fresh in my mind. In the case of *Pond* there resulted in me a different sense of inadequacy because of my own personal failure to lift a single word, or sentence, or paragraph from this writer's book in which to share with important others in my life, those being, for the most part, the good citizens who actually read what I might say after I may have read a particular book of common interest. I still cannot believe I failed to pilfer one word of hers for my own use until almost the very end. It was then that a phrase suddenly struck me, that being ...*no one can know what trip is going on and on in anyone else's mind*... and I abruptly stopped reading and immediately set to recording my own thoughts about my endless uphill battle in regards to developing some sort of intimacy with my father. Go figure, but that is what happened to me while I was reading. Not exactly a mind-bending phrase or slice of a sentence worthy of remembering, but from the moment it lit into me I was impelled to put my pen to paper, which is a good thing where I come from.

For whatever reason, that snippet from *Pond* led me to remember several snowstorms we had while growing up in northern Michigan. And it wasn't my memory of the snow fights and forts we built among all the frozen white piles dumped in the vast acreage near our home where the city deposited loads of snow removed from the roads in and around our small town. What I did choose to remember instead was the weekly city garbage truck that a man named Tippy Shanebeck drove around town with his son Benny riding on the back along, if memory serves, a friend named Ben Tarnosky as well as a rather menacing ex-felon by the name of Eddie Birdy. Eddie was said to have raped a young girl several years prior and we were all instructed to keep a safe distance from him and not stare too closely as he was bound to expose himself at some future date. But having a few years of memory weighing on me, and plenty of adult experience, I suspect that what we were told as kids often was not exactly true. But then, my renewed remembrance while reading *Pond* wasn't even about Tippy Shanebeck, or Benny and Ben, or even Eddie Birdy, but rather my older brother's and my responsibility to keep the family's driveway cleared of snow all winter, including the apron running out into the always-drifting road.

Keeping the driveway clear was, for the most part, doable because back then people had driveways sized enough for one large car like my mother's '57 Pontiac which she kept safely in the garage, or my father's company car which back then seemed to always be the latest model Chevrolet Impala. I looked back on the endless hard work and amount of time it took my brother and I to clear that apron, which according to our dad had to be shoveled out at an almost forty-five degree angle so our mother and he could both navigate their motored exits comfortably. The problem became for my brother and I the amount of snow that had fallen, or was yet to fall, or the storm that seemingly would never have any tapering off whatsoever. Our father taught us both to begin our work early and finish late so as to keep up with these great amounts in a more manageable exercise of endurance. There were days we shoveled for an entire day and the next one as well. And as much as we attempted to do a suitable job there was always the typical criticism from our father that we could have applied ourselves better, and we were again ordered outside in our boots and gloves and hats to clean up our mess and widen more the angled apron to his satisfaction. The worst part always came, inevitably, when the gigantic city dump trucks would come through and plow another abundant load across the entire swath we had already made clean and presentable. Sometimes there was more dumped snow than ever before as neighbors often just shoveled their own snow out into the road and the plows deposited theirs into our clean path as well. And that became a metaphor for me about what I chose to remember about my dad and how our intimacy never developed into anything more than keeping our shovels handy in which to clear and pile more heaps of mounting snow.

So, basically, *Pond,* though amazing, was a book seemingly about nothing but brimming with meaning. Every story felt as if you had been sitting there in the kitchen with Claire-Louise and she was relating perhaps insignificant details about her life to you but making them fully alive and always clever, charming, and extremely interesting. The more I learned of her proclivities the greater involved I became and thus grew more than enamored with her as a person of interest to me. The rhythm and lengths of her chapters (or stories, if you insist) flowed well and eased into each other, offering up a gait easy and comfortable enough to keep pace with. I also particularly enjoyed her use of a sophisticated vocabulary. Never did I deem her choice of words as pretentious or out of place with what she was accounting. But it is obvious the woman is gifted and smart and knows what she is talking about. Claire-Louise Bennett is much too talented not to be heard.

But in my particular case, I fear my personality may be found lacking. There have been occasions when I have felt somewhat popular among my peers, but too often the feeling is fleeting. Any significance awarded my personal financial gain and prosperity due to artistic efforts would result in unfavorable findings. But I rarely withhold counsel to any aspiring writer, and never resist the opportunity to express how important one's personality plays in establishing esteem and affinity from the strangers who might read us. It is difficult to continue reading any writer who bores us, who might be too enamored with himself, or think he better than he is. Humility, and a bit of humor, helps to ease the discerning reader into our creative world, one we must certainly call our own, or there would be little point in completing the exercise. The fact that I married a woman far above my own economic standing, that she was far more beautiful and sexy than I was, and that her academic education exceeded anything I had woefully attempted through my own self-manufactured studies, I would hope, lends some credence for my being a bit of a high achiever based on where I came from. My place of birth could provide enough eccentric characters for a full-length movie, but it takes more tact and ingenuity than simply setting names and behaviors on paper. I introduce again the name of Claire-Louise Bennett as a perfect example for what it takes, so much so that I often drop her name to those I love who seriously read. While my new daughter-in-law and her husband were visiting our cabin here in northern Michigan I used the opportunity to suggest for the second time this Booker Prize finalist as *the book to read*. Upon their return home to southern California she sent a photo of her latest purchase, *Pond,* and it being one of the two first books entered into her brand new Kindle. This new daughter-in-law of mine finds my old hometown quite interesting and she encourages my telling stories that include these fascinating family names. I doubt she has yet heard the entire list of names and events certain to follow as I continue on composing my historical artifacts. Two names I know I had failed to mention during her latest visit are my piano teacher Mrs. Kochendorfer, who kept her living room furniture covered in thick clear plastic and who sat too claustrophobically near you on the piano bench, and our next door neighbor Lutie O'Laughlin who unsuccessfully attempted to poison our little dog Frisky, a wire-haired fox terrier.

Chapter 12: Better Hurry Over with the Rope

About a week before our adult children were to
arrive at the cabin my parents came for a small
cookout. My mom and dad have lived in this
remote area their entire lives, and for the last
thirty-some years they have made my father's
childhood home their own. Both nearing their
nineties now, we attempt to at least be nice and
thoughtful, do good things, but keep our visits
with them as short as possible. They are both End
Days-Armageddon believers and use their church
and bible studies to fill their social calendar.
Their politics are extremely right-wing and
bat-shit crazy. And bigotry reigns. But as they
continue to age we confront them less and less
and allow them their idiotic views of what can

make our country great again.

My dad loves it when I make old-fashioned ribs
on my Weber grill, and when he found out we
were simply having hamburgers he was
disappointed, and told me so. But he ate the
burgers and was pleased, but never throughout
my life with them has there ever not been
complaints. My wife and parents were all sitting
down to eat on the original spruce picnic table we
had purchased over ten years ago from a neighbor
down the road named Elroy. He worked out of
his garage and fabricated wooden tables for the
numerous inland lake recreational communities
surrounding the area. After ten years of use our
table had seen better days, even though we had
painted it regularly and treated it with respect.
Made from spruce I knew the table would not last
forever, and it was evident that the rotting had
progressed. When we first arrived at the cabin
this summer I offered to build us a brand new
table, but my wife suggested we get one more
year out of this one. She bought a new can of
paint with plans to soon begin her summer
project. But her frugal idea turned out not to be a
very good one. As I sat down next to my mom to
eat my burger the support-end of my seat plank
abruptly snapped and down to the ground I went
in a hurry. I was worried my eighty-eight year old
mom would also soon be joining me so I
hurriedly, but gingerly, rose to my feet. But it
was only my end of the table which was
dry-rotted and punky as can be. The hanging
support joist broke clean in two as there was no
good wood at all within it. I managed to violently

tear the remaining length of the plank from off the other cross support and quickly set in place two lawn chairs for us to comfortably finish our meal. My dad sat across from us laughing his ass off at my misfortune as he is always wont to do when others suffer more than he. The next day I made a quick run to the lumber yard and the same day built a new and better table at which to take our meals when company comes to visit.

Chapter 13: Much Truth is Spoken That None May Be Revealed

What happened can be observed as having two outlandishly green and elongated, heavy-laden, unripened glands shoved abruptly into my face. Here he was, coming at me with crazed eyes wide and excitably happy, smiling as if he just won the booby prize he'd been waiting for all his life. It took both his hands to hold them. My neighbor Sally across the street had just asked if he wanted them, if his parents could use the squash, and he eagerly accepted them both and bubbly rushed back over. I was in hiding, rocking away, nestled in my favorite chair, some expensive Carolina wicker brand that we had been given, not exactly free I might add, as we had to pay the common carrier freight costs of $400 for them being boxed and hauled from Jackson Hole, Wyoming where my wife's sister was liquidating most all her belongings in order to join her husband on a sailboat. The man is a doctor wanting to retire and they devised a two-year plan to float around on that thing until he could come up with a better idea. In the meantime his wife would remain basically homeless until he was good and ready to settle back down. Not a big lover of men like that, but it is not my life to be concerned with. I was taking a break on the porch, out of sight behind our full-length matchstick blinds, safely concealed behind a porch screen that no one can reliably see into from outside. I was resting and rocking, temporarily free from entertaining family, a rather too-demanding activity of having three adult boys and their ladies visiting us at the same time. I already knew I would never do this again. They were here for an entire week and I suppose this gift of the squash was received by my son in the best interests of helping feed all of us, but I for one had wished he hadn't carted them over so quickly. My endeavors on the grill had become already a never-ending job and the week had just begun. For a brief moment I did consider that maybe the squash might be a good idea, but they were so huge and unnerving I wasn't sure what I could do with them. Sixteen inches of bulging dark-green protuberance would scare just about anybody not used themselves to mammary-type indulgences of this kind. And there were two of them which added to the reality of my shock and awe. It occurred to me that I was momentarily reliving a part of my past which included brief visits as a kid to my father's aging aunts off Duby Road in Alabaster, up on the sandy hill, whereupon introduction I would be uncomfortably squeezed between their bulging breasts and forced to hold my breath until freed and able again to gasp for precious air. Additional flashbacks of my private perusals in the woods gazing at photographs found in countless issues of damp National Geographic magazines also produced horrid memories of disgustingly enormous black elongated melons hanging off countless brown and piercing chests. But admitting to myself that grilled vegetables are very good if done properly kept these old nightmares temporarily at bay. Absent my horror, I knew regardless that any available space on my Weber would be limited when preparing meat for eight carnivorous adults. My wife had been busy inside the cabin engaged as a ban jee, baking desserts, using our two-week old Premier electric range as if she were preparing a personal audition for a Pillsbury Bake-off. Our lives had gone from slow, mundane-relaxing, to production-flurry chaos previously unexampled at this our summer cabin. Our eleventh summer here would be a celebration of creative cuisine, an extravaganza in the woods, and what I call a northern Michigan version of glorified camping.

Acquiring our new Premier range was long overdue as to upgrades needed since we first bought the cabin almost eleven years ago. We have had the same old range and refrigerator for all these years, and for certain they both worked well enough for the two or three months we annually live here. No complaints there. But they were so out of place in our small kitchen. Much too large for a six hundred square foot cabin. The refrigerator did have a small and annoying drip occurring when the weather turned hot and sticky, which lasted at most for two weeks or less so it was generally no big deal to speak of. But the high humidity rarely experienced in these parts did cause the outdated contraption to leak moisture, and I am certain it would have eventually rotted the floor beneath it. The fact that it hadn't already broken through over the last eleven years was probably due to a bit of luck and the flooring being of the old reliable linoleum that most people these days would have discarded and changed out years ago. Not us. My wife and I hate change and enjoy old things anyway. My wife even more than I. She goes in spurts, but too often she tends to bring home more old stuff than needed and I am forever scolding her like a child sometimes and imploring her to please stop this obsessive compulsion of hers for buying what I term junk. But these original two appliances were really too old and used-up to be effective anymore, and their styles were not conducive at all to our aesthetic bent. It seems that word aesthetic pops up often in descriptions of what I like, and more so its lack of, and is what tends to disrupt my temporary happiness enough to disgust me to no end. So we bought both appliances brand new from a Brooklyn-based outfit which offered the lowest prices as well as free shipping. A new apartment-size Premier range and LG bottom-freezer model arrived only days before our family visitors did, and my wife had been busy the last few days practicing her baking skills with this new oven that reminded me of a child's EasyBake. It certainly was cute, and we had happened just recently at a store in town upon a porcelain-topped base cabinet to fit exactly in between them.

Chapter 14: Doubting Love

But feelings, the ones generally unwanted, seem to always be the downfall of any family get-together, and this visit would be no exception. I gratefully accepted the squash and expressed my confidence that we could use them. But the unsightly swelling gibbosities remained in my ugly way all week, edged and finally shoved off to the side, and eventually placed by my sometimes vengeful wife in order to personally disrupt my revered space on the table that holds my 4-cup coffeemaker. After we bought the new appliances and found this cabinet to fit so perfectly between them we made a new and steadfast, in my opinion, household rule that the new workspace on top of the cabinet would be kept free of clutter, thus allowing the other table, situated halfway between the wall that held the kitchen sink and the one flanked with appliances, her own to make a personal mess of. But already too often I found myself reminding her of our new rule, and nothing irritates me more than her refusal to honor a sensible and fair arrangement. Of course, it is impossible for couples, and especially a group of people this size, to always remain happy. And it would be unrealistic to think that on a regular basis everyone would feel they are always being heard and fairly getting their way. A more reasonable world is actually chock full of compromise and our cabin would be no exception. But first there must issue forth complaints and disagreements, that with luck and a bit of effort, come to some resolution. In less healthy environments I suppose denial and indifference plays a more comfortable and meaningful role in which nobody feels anything and mouths remain shut.

Having our adult children and their female companions visiting is always wonderful. But for me, playing dad, husband, and friend while company visits is fraudulent at best as I am rarely completely present in that realm of reality. This particular event proved a bit of a postponement to my erotic fantasies regarding my wife which generally rule my life. I do exhibit enough

control over my virtual life that I maintain a
responsible adult-like ruse developed long ago at
the same time our children were born. All the
years managing a career and home were actually
quite easy for me, but true happiness, whatever
that is, has always remained slightly out of reach.
I have always desired more out of life than what I
earned from labor and a paycheck. Rarely have I
ever felt satisfied. But long years of hard work
and raising a family have not diminished my
tawdry desires still unrealized. Perhaps my
thinking may be construed by moralists as
shameful or indecent, but my desires are never
gaudy, or cheap in nature or appearance. My
erotic fantasies exist within the realm of the
highest class. When they include my wife they
are always celebratory in performance, and the
honor I bestow her are distributed in a
sophisticated spirit even in the most violent and
sweat-laden sex act imaginable. There is no end
to what my imagination provides me. This is
ultimately what I believe in, and what I live for.

But now these fucking squash gave me something
more to worry about. For over a week I have
maintained a low-grade headache and also
developed a sore throat, all of which I credit to
stress. I seem calm enough on the outside, but the
level of exhaustion I experienced after our
company went home was off the charts. It took
every bit of three solid night's sleep to ward off
the dull thud in my body and the extreme sense of
having been involved in a violent crash landing. I
think it came on me as total relaxation, and my
newfound sleepy enchantment was one I was

reluctant to extinguish any time soon. But eventually I did find a way back into my routine world of woodland hikes, our sparsely populated beach and gradual warming of Lake Huron, and a cabin so bovine and comfortable in the summer that I dream endlessly of never leaving it. But winter is a harsh reality. I grew up in northern Michigan. It is a season I prefer to now spend in Florida.

Chapter 15: Entertaining Suspicion

It was a bit surprising yesterday to receive an email from an insurance adjuster who informed me that an owner of one of the condominiums in our old complex in Louisville filed a claim for a leaking roof. We no longer own our unit as we sold it in the summer of 2015 to a young woman who was a royal pain in the ass to deal with. And I couldn't help but think she was the one who filed this claim as nobody else in the building would have done so. They would all know to call whomever is in charge of maintenance now and request having their roof repaired. Filing a claim would result in unnecessary paperwork and the homeowner's association dishing out a $5000 deductible. But based on what I know of this new owner she fits the mould for the typically demanding person who never cares about anybody but herself. But she would certainly be quick to tell you that she works with Ebola patients for the government in Africa. That was her excuse for never responding in a timely manner to any correspondence between us in getting our condo deal closed. It took over seventy days to get her mortgage finalized and closed, and my wife and I believed all along she was, on purpose, avoiding getting the lender the required proof of her employment and other documentation the bank requested. And because the homeowner's association still has not bothered to remove me from the online checking account that I previously managed for them I see she has yet to pay her first maintenance fee charge and appears to be already two or three months behind. Based on my disagreeable experience with her I sent an email warning the other owners she might be trouble, and have decided for my own health to stay as far away from that association as possible.

What occurred to me yesterday after I got that email was that bad news still affects me, even when the building is no longer partly mine. Over the past four years there have been a few instances of roofs springing leaks there, but never one over our unit, thank goodness. But nonetheless when it happened to somebody else I still felt responsible as I managed the business of running the association and getting the maintenance completed as needed. I had no choice but to take an active interest in the place as our own unit was a sizable investment, and we discovered that the company previously managing the building was bankrupting us. Our HOA account was almost dry and there was never any explanation of where our maintenance fees were going or what was getting done in our name. It appeared to all of us that no maintenance at all was being performed on our building so we fired them and I took over handling the job for no pay. When my wife and I finally escaped this disagreeable employ that summer of 2015 I was so relieved. I was tired of doing so much for people who never showed enough gratitude and would never lift a hand to help me. But yesterday my guts still roiled when I read there was a leak in the roof over somebody's living space. It will take me some time to get over feeling I am still responsible for that building. I forwarded the insurance adjuster's email to a couple of owners whose addresses I retained in my contact list. I really do not want to be bothered again by these people. No word yet from either of them, or even a thank you for letting them know about the problem.

Chapter 16: My Clock Cleansed

The two squash that did not fit among our plans became themselves harbingers. Having all three boys visiting along with their lady partners was tough enough. To explain the many differences and difficulties maintaining family harmony is a chore for me, and boring. And to make it interesting would ultimately hurt somebody's feelings. But differences exist even if nobody wants to admit them. Personal favorites and a certain comfort level cannot help but come into play. We are all subject to our environments. And we rely heavily on what we personally think we know as truth, and those opinions and ideas are sometimes restricted due to oppressive circumstances, and perhaps a fear for examining an experience too intensely. For example, when we are all together, my oldest son from my first marriage never totally feels a part of the group and comes across as jealous and resentful of the youngest son who is the only child my wife and I had together. Of course he denies his unhappiness vehemently, and always claims he is fine and it is myself who is looking for trouble. I have tried at least twice now to explain to this oldest one how raising this younger *only child*, and being around him daily for all his developmental years, makes for a bond stronger and quite unique than the relationship I have with my first-born. I did not raise him, and his mother who did is not the type of woman I now respect. I do love my first-born son but I will never have with him the type of relationship I have with my youngest one. It will always be different. Besides, by being raised by his mother, my oldest son is nothing like me. The few similarities that exist in our personalities includes a mutually dogged persistence and intensity for doing jobs well, and perhaps an unwarranted measure of insecurity in not being recognized and respected enough for our efforts. But this oldest son does not read the literature I do, nor does he write or look for art in the same way. Our aesthetic appreciations differ on almost every level. But we do enjoy involving ourselves in Detroit-area sports teams and will always have that in common. And that is what we must build our relationship on these days. Or we have agreed to, but often fail in our efforts because of perceived slights and jealousies that emerge when a larger group is involved. Even his wife is much different than the type of woman I am attracted to. But these two people are good for each other, and I am glad and wish them a long and happy life together, but I hold no pretensions for them ever fitting in specifically to the degree they want to. My stepson, my wife's first born, is another example of a fellow I spent an enormous amount of time getting to know and struggling through life with. We have shared so many experiences together, and he is a brilliant young man who has been successful in everything he tries. His new wife is the best woman he ever could have hoped for, and they openly spar with each other, pitting their personal wit and intelligence bare-fisted in the ring. I connected with this woman the very first time I met her. One day during their visit to our cabin she helped me cut up vegetables for shish kebobs, and we made our efforts into an art project as we slid the colorful delectables onto what felt like countless bamboo skewers. It was extremely time-consuming but also a great deal of fun working side by side. I can easily be intimate with her and risk saying things perhaps controversial and with meaning. In contrast, my oldest son and his wife need to be engaged in more exciting, high-speed activities and entertainment. Perhaps it has something to do with them living for so long a mere block off Venice Beach in California. The Hollywood scene has never interested me and I am put off by all the posturing aspiring actors and directors have to engage in in order to be noticed significantly. Physical enhancements are the norm and not the exception.

Our youngest son, himself a gifted photographer, is happy to float around in Lake Huron on an old-school inner tube. His new girlfriend is just like him. Occasionally they can be observed sitting off to the side engaged for example in his affectionate reading out loud to her J.D. Salinger's *A Perfect Day for Bananafish.* Though all three of our boys are obviously loved it was heartwarming to see the affection our youngest son's new mate expressed to him often. He is himself a hard man to deal with, a fourteen-year veteran of NYC, and it will take a special woman to love him properly. But the fact that she likes the books he does, and she loves him reading to her often, portends a promising future. I was warmed by watching them both floating around in the bay on those inner tubes. It reminded me of a time when I did the same. I was not surprised that this son of mine enjoys his leisure in similar ways that I used to, and so I made a secret pledge to myself that I would again engage in that practice after they left, that I would brave the waters of my great Lake Huron, and float about in carefree leisure, appearing to have a very good time. And I did. When their visit was over and they all returned to their respective homes, I hauled that tube religiously in the back of the Jeep, waiting for the right day, temperature, and waves, for me to take my plunge. But when the day finally came I realized I had forgotten how to hop on, how to fit my ass inside without tipping my craft over and getting water in my ears which had resulted in my ceasing to swim years ago. Swimming no longer was worth the constant earaches. But doused I was, dunked and drenched again in the waters of Lake Huron. I persisted however and never gave up in my quest to remember my old and practiced maneuver. I figured it out, finally, by paying strict attention instead to how I slowly got off that rubber tube, and then simply reversed myself as the proper way to get back on. The procedure was profoundly easy, and I felt again my old and confident self. And for several days in succession I embarked on my new watercraft, floating around like a duck and infidel, oblivious for that time about the world I am forced to adapt to as it always is changing around me.

Chapter 17: Beyond the Way of Return

Three weeks remained of our summer vacation
and we went to the beach every day. It felt good
to drive the thirteen miles or so through the forest
it took to get there. Tawas Bay Point State Park
is an amazing place. This year they are
celebrating fifty years of its existence. The
campground was built when my wife and I were
young kids, and the trees we both remember as
being no more than four feet tall and the place
originally looking like a desert. Neither of us
ever had any desire to camp there, and it took all
these many years for the trees to mature and for
the grounds to become shaded and cozy as can be.
But the beach was always beautiful. The nature
trail out to the point of land jutting into the bay
was an astounding ecosystem filled with deer and
turtles, frogs and birds. The beaches were filled
with flocks of what for all my life I knew as
seagulls. But what I discovered this summer was
a variety of bird unbeknownst to me. I have
known of the rare Piping Plover's nesting grounds
for the last several years due to all the birders
hiking the point with their cameras and

notebooks, generally looking like retired people, aging and easily entertained. But since moving to Florida I understand why they look so interested and happy as birds do tend to offer riveting entertainment. It is quite fun identifying every species and discovering a rare find from time to time. The Piping Plover is a rare bird that so happens to inhabit the beaches and marsh along this point of land extensively. It is not uncommon to have four or five of these little guys scampering along on their little feet, keeping a safe distance ahead of you as you make your way along the beach. And always surrounding you are the many gulls hanging about the sand and waters of Lake Huron. But *seagulls* they are not. It is perplexing to me why our local schools and teachers failed in their curriculum to ever mention to us the vast natural resources available to us in the area as outdoor classrooms. In fact, though the gulls do look quite similar, there are most often both Ring-billed Gulls and Herring Gulls gathered together in flocks along the shoreline. The Ring-billed Gull is the most prevalent here by numbers as large as three to one. But they sometimes mix together. Upon learning of their differences it was quite engaging to distinguish one from the other. They both look quite similar with their white heads and bodies spread with black-tipped gray wings. But the Ring-billed Gull has yellow legs and a black ring on the end of its yellow beak. In contrast, the Herring Gull has fleshy pink legs and a plain yellow bill. One photograph I took of a couple Ring-billed gulls this summer accidentally included another bird I had never seen before. The reason I hadn't noticed this bird while hiking the shoreline was because it blended in inconspicuously along with its gray feathers. But this strange bird in my photograph had a distinctive black head and brilliant red beak, which seen in the picture contrasted enormously with the white-headed Ring-billed Gull sporting its basically yellow beak with a black ring around the end of it. This strange bird inhabiting my photograph turned out to be a Caspian Teal which is a rare sighting, but does occur in its yearly migrations. The more I learn about the area I grew up in, the more perplexed I become at my teachers and parents failing to ever express their own excitement for living in such a wonderful natural area. For years growing up we heard about Tuttle Marsh and the monster that lived there. Occasionally there would be an incident reported where a young lady on a spooked horse might get thrown because of this reclusive strange jack-in-the-box big foot living in the marsh off Wilbur Road. And for the first time in my sixty-two years I visited the marsh this summer. It was not an easy place to find, but when we did happen upon this natural treasure my wife and I were amazed we had never been there before nor ever really heard anything accurate about it. It is a protected area owned by our Agriculture Department. Something like 365 acres contain this ecosystem that includes as many as 370 species of birds, as well as turtles, frogs, beaver, and who knows what else. I am simply flabbergasted by the ignorance of the people in charge of our instruction and development as human beings.

Chapter 18: In Shadow Like a Death Mask

Of late, in my independent reading study, I have subjected myself to numerous mundane and verbose works. Because of my slightly depressing literary summer boredom I decided to pull from my cabin shelf a title I had previously read at least two times. *The Walk* by Robert Walser was first translated into English by Christopher Middleton in 1957. In 2012, New Directions published a contemporary translation by Susan Bernofsky which included Walser's significant revisions and added text made after its initial publication. It is a charming tale and Walser spares no punches in his relating of it. Near the end of the book the main character, a struggling writer, is required to meet with a revenue official regarding his failure to pay income taxes and explain why it appears to most he does not have to work due to his leisurely lifestyle of walking and daydreaming everyday.

Do you realize that I am working obstinately and tenaciously with my brain, and am often perhaps in the best sense active when I present the appearance of a simultaneously heedless and out-of-work, negligent, dreamy, idle pickpocket, lost out in the blue, or in the green, making a bad impression, apparently devoid of any sense of responsibility?

For those of us who take long walks or ride our bicycles extensively it comes as no surprise the comforts and delights Walser describes available to the enchanted lover of invigorating lore found in nature and country. It is quite obvious that Walser himself believes his craft is not enough respected, and shoddy reviewers and hacks can cause great harm to any serious writer already impoverished and living frugally. He pleads to this official that his taxes be reduced to the lowest rate possible.

There accompanies the walker always something remarkable, something fantastic, and he would be foolish if he wished to let this spiritual side go unnoticed; by no means, however, does he do this, but rather cordially welcomes all peculiar phenomena, becomes their friend, their brother; he makes them into formed and substantial bodies, gives them soul and structure just as they too for their part instruct and inspire him.

It is both soothing and fantastical to allow the mind to run free on a walk through an easy forest or sandy coastline where Walser writes *chaos begins and the orders vanish.* His instruction insists there is a *sweet song of departure* among these *solid technicians.*

As the walk nears its end and darkness overcomes him, his thoughts turn lamentable and fill him with regret. He is alone now with self-reproof, his heart a burden to him as rain rustles gently down the leaves. With what seems to him now tears, the drama of his former life opens, and all his miserable failures occur to him. He knows he has been remiss in expressing his honest devotion to her, and regrets now he never said, "I love you."

I thought of a beautiful girl...and a poor, forsaken man...and nausea took hold of me.

Chapter 19: The Death of a Beekeeper

For two years I postponed reading *The Death of a Beekeeper* written by a Swede named Lars Gustafsson and published first in 1978. The subject is a man attempting to live within his own terminal disease and the mounting pain associated with it. Westin *has refused to surrender the time left him to the impersonality of a hospital, preferring to take his fate upon himself, to continue his solitary, reflective life in the Swedish countryside.* I avoided reading *The Death of a Beekeeper* because I felt the subject matter would somehow advance my own impending death. I certainly have no desire to contract a terminal disease, nor do I wish to hear from a doctor something about me that would enforce me changing my lifestyle. There are always minor health concerns that require attention. And it is inevitable that something will eventually occur. *The Death of a Beekeeper* generally involves Westin dealing with his terminal sentence on his own terms. It is a meditation on avoiding the hospital, living with pain, and harboring a secret festering and growing within one's body. After reaching the halfway mark I had not discovered anything earth-shattering or even helpful to any condition I may eventually find myself faced with. As with eating out, and trying new restaurants, I am for the most part usually disappointed in the fare. My anticipation is always contrary to what actually transpires. But how can a person approach anything without favorable expectations and a desire for it to be successful? It proves how hard it is to write, and how important it is to stay focused on the object from start to finish. I felt the author Gustafsson rambled, and I do like digression, but he failed to connect any dots for me. Too often the entries in his journal, that also included his fictions, seemed foreign to the basic ideas behind his main text. I do enjoy an unrelenting supersaturation absent of any repentance. Lars Gustafsson's *The Death of the Beekeeper* could have remained constantly focused on his character Westin's cancer, its pain and discomfort, his living with it on a daily basis, and what his life had become for him now as he looked back into what he had made of his past instead of the other unnecessary and often silly narratives he proffered.

Chapter 20: An Old Dog Barking

Why might a person do as they do? In short, maybe *for meaning*. Another answer takes much longer to explain. I hold art responsible. My creating of it. I confess to also using my obsessive desire for my wife to further my artistic ambitions. When a personal act, in the religious sense of *sinning*, is even slightly considered, my blood rises quickly to greet it. Life becomes more heightened, alive, imminent, and taken less for granted. That which is emotionally arousing results in greater clarity than being involved in what is mundane. How vividly we actually remember something from the past determines our continued memory of it.

But my childhood and adolescence still haunt me. My greatest sin of omission is my continued failure to properly attack those strict institutions of instruction and religion that attempted to mould me as a young boy, institutions which obviously still hold some sinister power over me. And I am referring to those self-proclaimed holier-than-thou authorities who still hide behind their veil of spiritually-distant goodness. This same holy blessedness deceitfully promised to be bestowed on me through some pontifical action depending wholly upon my acceptance of their godly beliefs. I despise those teachers for all the guilt and shame they have inflicted, and still do to new victims. And for my initial wanting so much to believe in them, or what turned out to be my futile attempts to do so, and for all those days of my prior existence, once freely given to me from birth as my own life to live, now lost forever to these oft-inflicted assaults of guilt and shame.

Chapter 21: A Careless Roar Begins Where the Highway Ended

Recently I have read some articles that attempt to explain Gordon Lish's teaching method and how he demanded his students to seduce him. I was certainly aware of this, but still it was refreshing to read of it again. It is what I do. In my poetry I attempt to enter the abyss Lish so often spoke of in class, and if I fail at my efforts and not succeed, I wish at least to come to the edge of this precipice in which my balance, or my lack of such, might allow me to hover a bit on the brink or tumble freestyle into the darkest of my blackened pits. And this was the first involvement in Lish's so-called *jeopardy*, and in that, history must, and will agree I did succeed. But the same good fortune has been absent in my prose fiction, and thus, my life story has become what I choose instead to save for history, if there is to be any.

In my poems I sought to seduce him. Many years ago, before the turn of this 21st century, after meeting for a few minutes in our room at the Washington Square Hotel, the three of us made our way back down the narrow stairwell of the hotel and my wife later told me how Gordon's hand brushed across her breast at the moment he casually mentioned to her how vain he was even in his advancing age. When we returned home to Kentucky I decided to encourage her, in the future, to respond to him with kindness and attentive concern instead of distancing herself from him out of respect for me and the sanctity of our marriage. So then, and simply for fun, not only did she tease my avowed interest in having her eventually bed him, but she then devised nude photo shoots we might make of her and then she chose specific prints we might then mail to him in packets from our home so far away. She sometimes included little written notes that honestly confessed she was trying to get beyond her Christian upbringing and the doctrines she had learned, though long ago had rejected as her own. She was now, in truth, attempting to create herself as a woman reborn, and to make art alongside the poet and the teacher who made up this group of three. This triangle was eventually, as planned, to be the climax of a long and fruitful relationship. It was to be the last act to a gratifying story, and a consummation of the love we all shared for each other. And because he was infamous in his womanizing, and his own fictions tend to obsessively prove it, I asked my wife to become another one of his concubines, a conquest he might talk of and perhaps make his too-public remarks about how lovely she was and how lucky I was to have her. And the only reason she ever considered in our marriage to having sex with somebody other than myself was because I asked her to. It began as a favor to me as a way to thank Gordon for all he had done. The poet I had become would simply not have evolved if it were not for the teaching and friendship of Gordon Lish. And at times it was troubling to me that I had produced this possible event to come, but it was never wrong of me to have had these fantasies. And the dangers of our dirty dancing made our love life wonderful. Our excitement grew with each new idea of how we might seduce him, again and again, and at times, for our own selfish pleasure.

Chapter 22: Tongues of the Wild Beasts

These days it is difficult remembering. At least
experiences in reliable order. And my fantasies,
both sexual and literary, have played such a huge
role in my life that I doubt now almost everything
I relate back to myself through my written words
on the page. Nevertheless, I muster on. Thanks
to these sharp remembrances of some
relationships still prevalent in my mind I am able
to retain a few treasures. But what really
occurred, or what is or is not the truth, the reader
must decide. And perhaps this will result in an
insignificant maculation. A mere tainting of our
flowered nest. But at this late period in my life,

and the state of the world I find myself present in, I simply do not care. I recently discovered the Austrian writer Elfriede Jelinek, who appears to have no shame and is willing to expose everything in her writing in the hope something in her own world might change. She is brutally honest in her fiction and she often gives pause for us to reconsider our own. Her novel *Lust* comes directly to mind as one of her boldest works. The counsel she offers writers is to always maintain, at all costs, the status of the outsider.

Chapter 23: The Permanent Impairment of My Vision

Over the course of the summer of 2014, I re-read a book originally published in the seventies titled *Sunshine* in which I surprisingly discovered there was no resolution at the end. Not exactly a great or novel phenomenon, nor something required of any book in order that I might enjoy more my reading of it. But what remained puzzling and somewhat disconcerting for me was the total lack of any final ending appropriate to what I had thought I remembered and had now again taken what was left of my valuable time to read, perhaps a bit too thoughtfully and focussed for my own good. But this was the very latest assignment I had created for myself, and I always apply myself to being the best student possible even if I am the only participant present in my self-taught class. Suffice to say that at the end of the novel a young boy named Freddy remains in hiding under a kitchen table as his crazy father in a wheelchair brandishes a cast iron poker at anyone who moves near enough for him to get a decent swipe. The most important development in the book had already occurred as the male and female pair of black hired help gradually rise up against this cripple, a racist Southern master of the 70's, and threaten to quit his suffocating employ. Even before the book's end the boy's mother has gone insane and been sent to an asylum, finally escaping her own house hell-bent for ruin. But previous to having been taken away to her padded room, this mother had also cheated on her husband with their black handyman, same as her husband had cheated on her by copulating with the housekeeper. Freddy, the young and frightened son, is a witness to all of this from one of his several hiding places around the house and grounds of their Florida plantation, or two-story leaking clapboard structure it has gradually become. Throughout the duration of the book, the daily torrential rains threaten to never end their downpours, and little hope ever remains that anything will ever change. Somehow the torrential rains, the incessantly crazy chatter, the various copulations, and always mounting fear, are all connected to what must follow as regards my personal recounting.

Chapter 24: Dark Waters of a Dream

Sartre was infatuated by the theater of seduction, and he knew it. He described it as a "literary labor", which, much like his writing, involved fine words, adroit sentences, and skilled use of viewpoint. Hazel Rowley, *Tête-à-Tête*

After reading the first six pages of *Sunshine*, now fifteen years or so after my very first introduction to this title, I find little to remind me of why I had thought Gordon Lish was the actual author behind this rather insane book. Names such as Baby Ruth, Poop-Pa, Monkey Ward and Mr. Talking Frog seem now to be almost absurd to the Gordon I have come to know after over twenty years working with him personally. Though I began sending him my versions of fiction beginning in 1987 it wasn't until the summer of 1995 when I attended my first Fiction-writing Class on the campus of Indiana University in Bloomington that I got a taste of what it might be like to actually become friends with him. Of course, the first thing he wanted from me was his exorbitant fee paid, my personal check, but that was the last money I ever spent as a student as he refused in subsequent years any further attempts of payment from me. The violent energy he exhibited when he first saw me sitting there in class, the way he came at me so forcefully, questioning me with no introduction, reaching out his hands exuberantly, enquiring of me as to the whereabouts of his check, if I had it for him, and if I was prepared to hand it over, was enough to convince me that this was no ordinary man I was being confronted by. But I pretty much already knew all this as I had previously read his first book of short stories titled *What I Know So Far* which, for me, was nothing short of miraculous.

Lately, there has been a shift in contemporary literature, at least in our country, where the emphasis is made, it seems, on a clever use of language instead of simply relating a great story, made-up or otherwise. I do not believe Gordon Lish has been wholly responsible for this. These days I mostly read foreign works in translation, and what began for me as a practice in which I read authors writing in their native German, French, and some Spanish has now developed into a serious need to also study Scandinavian prose. Writers publishing in our country today, who claim to have been influenced by Gordon Lish, produce for the most part silly works of inconsequential agendas that are, for me, in some ways, coded and tiresome. Missing from these present-day offerings are great performances the likes of, say for example, a Lish-made Raymond Carver. I never thought that one day I would desire to be removed from my connection to the School of Lish, but sadly it has happened for me. But to be fair and forthcoming, as I have claimed already numerous times, I would be nothing of a poet without him and I would also not even know how to read these great foreign works I discover now on an almost daily basis. Gordon Lish is responsible for my development, and even my distancing of myself from those who wish to still align themselves with this so-called School of Lish, an institution that Lish himself refuses to endorse.

The voice of the narrator in Clifford Hagen's *Sunshine* is one of a child's even though an adult is speaking. Gordon employed the same affectation in his novel *Peru*. The sing-song voice and spontaneously rapid thoughts that an excitable kid might display become front and center. It immediately sets the opening tone of the book in only the first few pages. I remember remarking after having read Lish's *Peru* that I had never been more inclined to smell and feel my childhood than when engaged in reading this book. No other writer had ever brought my childhood back to me so vividly as Gordon Lish, and thus, I have always held *Peru* in high esteem. For me the book became the standard for what a great novel dealing with childhood should accomplish. Lish's use of repetition plays such an enormous role in his making of *Peru*. The key characters are not many, but Gordon continuously returns to each of them, circling each as if they were wagons on the plains and he was leading a party of bloodthirsty savages attacking this makeshift fortitude sure to surrender or perish in its attempts to protect itself. Our defenses are many when it comes to memory, and Gordon certainly has a way of disarming an enemy and getting to this hidden truth. But only on his pages of fiction. Gordon himself rarely lets anyone enter into his real world, never relaxing his own defenses or allowing his guard to be let down. He seems to always be in control in any social gathering, even within a casual, but personal, visit inside his home.

Chapter 25: Emotional Seduction

Though my expectations are less than positive, my second time reading through *Sunshine* seems to be going rather well. But only eleven pages in is obviously not a fair sample in which to judge what is to come. Still, there is every indication that the book may hold up as an accomplished work of fiction. What is amazing to me, even after all these years have passed, is that no physical sign of Clifford Hagen has ever surfaced outside the pages of this book. It really is as if Clifford Hagen literally disappeared. I remain confident the text was written under a pseudonym and by the time I am finished reading this novel, and my online research is complete, I am hopeful something will reveal itself. In the meantime I will enjoy learning more about Freddy and his father in the wheelchair and the insane family dynamics sure to take place. I believe this *rat tat tat* of rapid-fire chatter is preparing me. Already survivor's-guilt has reared its ugly head due to the sudden death of Freddy's brother. Shame and blame seem to thrive in this family's environment. Gordon often spoke in his fiction-writing class how he was defined in his own writing by the *shame* he carried. His best friend, the writer Don DeLillo, in contrast and according to Gordon, has been influenced by his personal feelings of *dread* made manifest in his writing. Both details seemed quite believable and logical to me, and therefore provides another clue that at that time the author of *Sunshine* was in fact Gordon Lish.

Is it possible that Clifford Hagen actually disappeared from off the face of the earth? Yesterday I spent an hour looking for him online. For any trace. And all I could discover was a piece in the *Kirkus Review* posted around the time *Sunshine* was published and also a review in the NY Times. *Harper & Row* was Hagen's publisher, which was no small coup for Clifford

Hagen, this being his first book. But Gordon Lish himself suffered a long and tumultuous relationship with *Harper's* in which his troubles with them have been substantially documented. Little Freddy sported an erection this morning in one of the pages I read of *Sunshine*, and I couldn't help but think of Gordon as being the creator of this character. The voice is so familiar, but not as hard now to accomplish given that I, and others, have also done the same thing in our own fictions for one reason or another. It is fun at times to be a little loose and insane on the page. It is, if nothing less, a wonderful exercise and a vehicle in which to blow off steam. Here little Freddy is rubbing his hardening penis as the black maid enters the picture and who then carries the boy upstairs to wash his face. The housekeeper's name is Baby Ruth and she has not become so familiar that she is remembered, or the reader has the slightest recollection of what she looks like. There have already been too many visitors to this ramshackle home because of the earlier abrupt and unexplained death of Freddy's brother.

KIRKUS REVIEW Pub Date: Jan. 13th, 1970
Publisher: Harper & Row

Little Freddy, to put it kindly, is disturbed -- with symptoms including low-grade sadism, voyeurism, ducking under tables in moments of uneasiness, and compulsive narration in a floodtide stream-of-consciousness style. But then his Miami environment isn't the healthiest either: Poop-pa, though paralyzed from the waist down,

*manages sado-masochistic wheelchair sex romps
with his grotesquely fat, malevolent nurse, Baby
Ruth, who also looms large in Freddy's real or
imagined erotic life and sidelines with Poop-pa's
black male attendant Jo Jo, who in turn had a
fling with the lady of the house -- before she
committed suicide and after Freddy's younger
brother died (of poisoning?). This should be
approached, if at all, in a diagnostic spirit. For
starters we suggest traumatic premature exposure
to Faulkner, Tennessee Williams, etc.*

And from the NY Times January 10, 1971:

*"Sunshine" is a mingling of
stream-of-consciousness, fantasy and first-person
narrative radiating from a precocious little boy
named Freddy, who lives with his family on one
of Florida's coasts. Freddy's folks are culled from
the Southern literary tree that sprouted so many
grotesques we have come to know and love. In
Mr. Hagen's hothouse are Poop-pa, a paralyzed
big daddy in a wheelchair; mama, who is no
better than she seems; Baby Ruth, a practical
nurse and maid of all work; and Jo-Jo, Poop-pa's
male orderly. As filtered through Freddy's
sensitive perceptions, the members of this
real-life quartet pursue one another in a
Freudian round robin (complete with once-exotic
sexual acts) that includes Mr. Talking Frog and
Captain Jim—obsessions from color TV. Freddy
may be an overly sophisticated observer for a
mere tad—but disbelief is suspended in the
Caligari cabinet of imaginative distortions the*

author has created.

Chapter 26: A Place of Fly-Specked Mauve Walls and High-Vaulted Ceilings

Sometimes Freddy gets a bit too excited and begins relating incidents that come too fast and numerous. In short, Freddy piles on. It all begins to sound like crazy talk after a page or two, and at times it is a reminder of the last few times I attempted to speak to Gordon on the telephone. Because he is more than eighty years old and has been battling skin disease or cancer for most of his life, and claims he ingests so many drugs to combat what amounts to dreadful ailments, that there are often occasions when he seems a bit discombobulated. Occasionally he mumbles and speaks as if he is heavily sedated. He does use sleeping pills and often stays up half the night before passing out or falling into a very deep and drug-addled sleep. For years he could maintain regular physical activity whether that meant attending the rare social function or when he, purportedly, would be engaged in fucking all night a woman he had some previous arrangement with. For Gordon, after he retired, he proclaimed to myself, and others, that sexual activities became even more important than even his writing. In conversations with me he decidedly wanted to be regarded as a marathon man in his sexual prowess, just as he had taught his fiction-writing classes lasting six to ten hours a session with no potty breaks or refreshments of any kind. (He later told me in a rare moment of complete honesty that he used a pill to help hold his water and suppress any need to use the restroom.) In his later years, after turning seventy, he expressed to me that going forward his new art form would be sex, and he performed these exercises with as many willing participants as could be made available to him. He consistently asked his associates for any of their discarded women, or any female acquaintance of theirs willing to go the sexual distance with him.

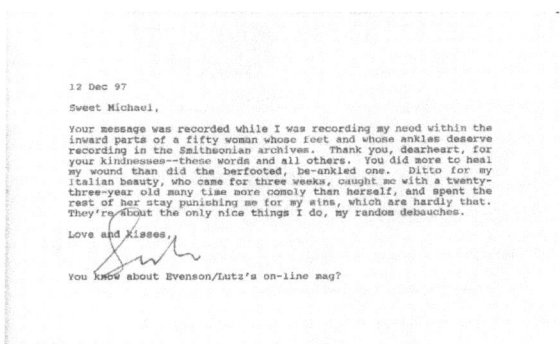

12 Dec 97

Sweet Michael,

Your message was recorded while I was recording my need within the inward parts of a fifty woman whose feet and whose ankles deserve recording in the Smithsonian archives. Thank you, dearheart, for your kindnesses--these words and all others. You did more to heal my wound than did the berfooted, be-ankled one. Ditto for my italian beauty, who came for three weeks, caught me with a twenty-three-year old many time more comely than herself, and spent the rest of her stay punishing me for my sins, which are hardly that. They're about the only nice things I do, my random debauches.

Love and kisses,

You know about Evenson/Lutz's on-line mag?

Sunshine harps and squeals in an incessantly endless rant, which for me, when I first read it, was a new and freeing literary experience. In addition, Gordon's own way of verbally going on and on in his eccentric and frightfully Jewish way was something else I had not heard before due to growing up in the stifling Lutheran Midwest. And as a teenager I read many classics while also searching for answers through the writings of Herman Hesse. Prior to my literary relationship with Lish and Hagen I mostly read for enjoyment many American westerns and detective novels.

From that lighter smorgasbord my reading
evolved into what would be extensive
introductions to Lish contemporaries such as
Thomas McGuane, Jim Harrison, and the much
younger Rick Bass. Gordon's fiction was so
novel to me that I was completely engaged in my
reading of it. But then, after no few years of it,
that voice with its typical accounting got old.
After a long history of pouring through all of his
work I began to see how some of it really was not
as good as I thought it once to be. *Peru* is a prime
example. Still a very good book, but not the
masterpiece I originally had labeled it as being.
Even Gordon's later collection of short stories
titled *Goings* should not have been published.
Better to have left his body of work at rest and
returned to his latest purported art form of
fucking. But it is possible his stable of willing
women had shrunk because of his advancing age
and declining popular interest in his literary
endeavors. No longer was Gordon as much in the
public eye as provocateur and trouble-maker. Not
long ago Gordon announced to me that he had
renewed his teaching activities and was back to
writing fiction again. He told me when he again
suited up that his sole purpose was to find new
women to fuck. Not the worst motivation, but
something he should have thought out further. His
literary oeuvre has suffered due to a bloated
perversion of his obsession.

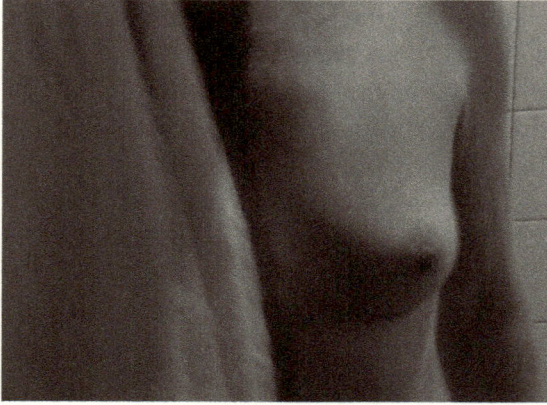

Chapter 27: The Unheard Music of the Spheres

Freddy obviously watches too much television. I am not surprised that this dysfunctional family relies on TV for entertainment and also as a babysitting service. It is so convenient to simply plop your child in front of the television, put in a movie, and *presto!* you have an hour or two of free time away from the kid. Gordon told me he relied on the television for all his news. He said the Discovery Channel was his favorite source for information regarding the world. That and porn. He loves porn. He uses it as instructional videos for the women who come to visit him. He calls these women his *cleaning ladies*. Mostly, he says, *they keep his pipes clean.* Gordon does his own housework. On his hands and knees scrubbing away and picking out lint behind the stove and refrigerator and anywhere else the stuff might find a place to hide. He claims there are entire days he spends cleaning. He does keep his apartment immaculate. And I imagine he attends to his women visitors with the same attention to detail he exacts in cleaning his house. I am sure he *gets* into every nook and cranny, and then, when finished with them, they all feel quite attentively preened and well manicured. His latest sexual activities have become an art form, he says, and something he has kept secret from his extended family. But for some reason he tells almost everybody he comes in contact with about these sexual activities. However, Gordon is always about appearances, making them, and controlling their outcomes.

The TV weatherman is reporting an impending hurricane and suddenly everyone in Freddy's household is scurrying around tying things down. Jo-Jo, the black caretaker, is busy nailing sheets of plywood over the windows as Freddy and his wheelchair-bound father do their best to assist him. Obviously, they do not help much. Anything that Jo-Jo might construe as a helpful benefit provided by these two people is anything but, and instead more insane chatter. It is a similar level of excitement, in fact, to once, while my wife and I were strolling with Gordon and his lady friend in Greenwich Village near the campus of New York University, Gordon's date caught her heel between some old cobble stones that made up the street that cuts through the university's faculty housing. She tripped and stumbled and Gordon caught her and exclaimed frantically, "Catherine, Catherine, are you all right, Dear?" His voice registering a panicky high note and expressing an urgency that sounded more grandmotherly than manly. He hysterically repeated this expression again, and perhaps for our benefit. Of course, we never did let on to Catherine or Gordon how thrilled we were to witness first-hand these hysterics of his. Later that evening, and many others to follow, my wife and I related the incident to each other remarking how caring and attentive Gordon most likely is in the presence of a lady. There were times my wife even imagined herself being attended to by Gordon Lish, and it seemed to both of us an interesting and surprisingly comfortable thought. So much attention and concern focussed on one person is quite romantic to some, my wife included.

Chapter 28: As Sure as God Made Little Owls

Poop-pa is the name of Freddy's disabled father. He sits in his wheelchair most of the time, but every now and then he actually stands on his own two legs, and even drives away in his car to get supplies before the big hurricane strikes. Poop-pa is attended to by the caretaker Jo-Jo and the very fat and voluptuous nurse slash cook slash housekeeper Baby Ruth. These are all rather crude people. Even the local police in this novel are as racist as Freddy and his dad. I am quite surprised at how little I remember from the first time reading this book except for the tone and craziness so abundant on these pages. It seems I would remember a bit more from my previous reading of several years ago, but I do not. This development does not bode well for the long haul facing me this summer. But Hagen's writing is interesting enough that early each morning here at my cabin I look forward to reading the required two pages before putting my pen to paper. I have learned from past experience that a regimented daily practice of discipline will produce a generally favorable result.

Gordon once related to me a story from his past when as an active father he would take his young son Atticus a half a block from their apartment building to Central Park to play and climb trees. The youngster was determined to climb a particularly large trunk of a tree that he could not quite get his legs around. Instead the boy would press his knees into the trunk in order to shimmy up the tree. But that proved impossible as well even though Atticus refused to quit trying. It wasn't until his knees and legs were all bloodied and it was time to return home that this obsession would stop. Gordon told me he filmed the entire incident. Even as an adult Atticus had a short career as a martial arts kick boxer and I managed, through the internet, to acquire a videocassette of one of his fights. The bout lasted three rounds and Atticus lost. Had the fight gone on another round I believe Atticus would have gotten the better of his opponent. There is no quit in Atticus Lish and his efforts are incessant and tiring to any opponent. And this persistence goes hand in hand with Gordon's teaching. Most people do give up if they do not succeed in a given time appropriate to each one's character. Some call my own character stubborn, and perhaps I am. I call it persistence. And I also learned long ago that what others think about, even if it pertains to me, is actually none of my business.

Of course, as in any sordid tale concerning a debauchery in the South, Freddy's mother is upstairs having sex with Jo-Jo while her husband Poop-pa is off in the car buying groceries before the storm. Jo-Jo is the black helper who boards up all the windows, stands on tall ladders, and perhaps takes too many chances by reaching out too far. He is sexually involved with Freddy's mother simply because he can be. Or the storm brings out a passion and sensuality of an animal nature typically not present in the course of their normal mundane days. In any case Freddy's mother and Jo-Jo are engaged in some heavy

love-making and Freddy can hear them,
especially the sound of his mother's cries as Jo-Jo
has his entire face aggressively planted between
her legs performing a major overhaul on her
genitals. There is nothing like a good
pornography to wake one from a typically banal
day. For years one of my long-distance services I
provided Gordon from my home in Louisville
was to search the internet for specific
pornographic artists and films he was interested in
acquiring. I purchased DVD's with one of two
credit cards of his I kept on file expressly for this
purpose. It was only in the last few years,
especially after my fall from the roof of my cabin,
that I quit doing this for him, or he stopped
asking. Up until this time Gordon reported to me
his every sexual conquest almost as they
happened. His proudest moment came when he
turned seventy-five and had the opportunity to
pull off a threesome.

Chapter 29: Long Slurring of the Bow

When Poop-pa returns home with the groceries and is putting them away he asks Freddy what his mother has been up to. Freddy tells his father that while he was out shopping he saw Jo-Jo upstairs licking at her crotch. Nothing more was said. At least not right away. Perhaps after Poop-pa has time enough to think about it some his mind won't sit so well with this graphic visual. But then, it is possible that this behavior is acceptable and generally a regular occurrence in their home. *Sunshine* was published in 1971 so it is possible that the idea of an open marriage was, or could be considered. The sexual revolution of the sixties in the decade prior to the publication of this book was an uprising rooted in a shared belief in the detrimental impact of sexual repression. The movement's conviction held that the erotic should be celebrated as a normal part of life and should not be repressed by family, industrialized sexual morality, religion, or the state. Many feminist thinkers believed the assertion of the primacy of sexuality would be a major step towards the ultimate goal of women's liberation, thus women were urged to initiate sexual advances, actually enjoy sex, and experiment with new forms of sexuality.

There did not seem to be any sudden anger from Poop-pa upon hearing of his wife's adventure with the black caretaker. There was no outburst typically resulting from such a marriage betrayal, so it is not beyond my understanding to accept these actions as being conducted among willing participants. Adultery is such an egregious crime to most couples in a relationship, or it often appears to be so on the surface. After consulting

Gordon over what had become an almost common occurrence in his own life, and what felt to me as my own unnatural and rather perverted thinking, Gordon counseled me that *all men fantasize their wives or girlfriends being fucked by someone other than themselves.* He added that it is *completely normal to have these thoughts.* And for years I maintained these fantasies, and even took measures in which the likely possibility might, in due time, favorably occur. According to the *Journal of Couple and Relationship Therapy*, approximately 50 percent of married women and 60 percent of married men will have an extramarital affair at some time in their marriage. And since it is unlikely that the people having affairs are married to each other in every case, the current statistics on the percentage of married couples who cheat on each other perhaps amounts to someone having an affair in nearly 80 percent of marriages.

Chapter 30: A Finger on a String

Freddy has a homemade hunting tool he calls his crab stick that he uses to beat the hell out of sand crabs on the beach. Jo-Jo does not like that Freddy does this and he threatens him with myths in which to scare him. Myths such as how a Giant Crab will crawl out of the water and on to shore and go after him for being so mean. But Freddy in no way curtails his destructive behavior. Freddy appears to be a troubled child. He no longer attends school as do the other children living here in this Gulf beach community. Since his brother died of what Freddy calls the *Black Plague* there have been no other children present in his life. Just Freddy alone among the misfits of his family. And it's a good bet his father Poop-pa is scamming the federal government with his wheelchair act, drawing a disability check from social security and whatever other payments he might also get on the dole. This is not a novel idea, but is the only instance of it happening in a book I have read. The day to day activities of Freddy are rather typical of many poor families. The TV still is the entertainment center, and children witness far too much of what dysfunctional adults engage in. Freddy's family life is seedy and it seems, unfortunately, the entire clan wants it to remain so.

For Freddy every day resembles a theater production. A troublesome life viewed from what seems a safe enough distance, seen through the eyes of a young and undeveloped child still relying on the care and nurturing of mature and responsible adults. And Freddy certainly knows his family is flawed. He also believes he does not need schooling like the other children in his Gulf community. He relies on his own familiarity with television celebrities such as the country and western star Hank Williams in addition to a book he calls the *Holy Bible* in order to draw references in the midst of the shattering events happening often around him. The storm and rains outside are observed by Freddy just as the trials inside his home are, and he manages them exactly the same way. Freddy copes with it all by witnessing and articulating what he sees as precisely as he can. He seems to speak for everyone. The evidence presented proves he cannot trust any of these adults, but he is so young he still needs them to care for him. So he somehow gets through it all by adapting to the circumstances as best he can, returning to his sofa and TV, and by murdering sand crabs with his special killing stick. He is not afraid of the purported Giant Sand Crab that wants to supposedly eat him as Jo-Jo claims it does. Freddy himself is out for blood, and with a vengeance meant to clear his head and release him from his daily dreadful existence.

Chapter 31: The Cheat Grass and Bitter Salt Cedar

The Florida Gulf Coast is a very strange place. And Freddy and his family are no exception. A constant feeling of dread is present on every page of this book as the hurricane continually threatens its coming destruction. Pounding rains add strict shifts in color to the beaches as the waves, normally nonexistent in the Gulf, erupt in massive size and violence crashing upon the shoreline. The hardiest ones among these residents seem to disregard these storms and instead practice a ritual of staying put and riding them out. Freddy, a frightened little boy, unfortunately, is among them.

I expect low-life and uneducated behavior out of Freddy as he taunts Baby Ruth with racial slurs calling her "Nigger, Nigger, Nigger." Poop-pa, in his wheelchair, does read the newspaper, though most likely it is a small-town rag or one of the national corporate-owned conglomerates that publishes a newspaper more patterned to the less sophisticated reader than say the NY Times. These dumbed-down newspapers focus on the typically dim-witted citizen that responds most heartily to nationalism and communities where publicly displayed examples of patriotism become more important than having a clean heart. Neighborhoods where flags are flown for all the world to see proclaiming in unison *USA! USA!* But this hasn't occurred yet in this story. Only the taunting of Freddy calling his caretaker Baby Ruth *Nigger* and his attempts to then escape her claws as she works herself into a slather to catch him. Why he also calls her a *dirty nigger whore* is failed to make clear, but perhaps Freddy has problems greater than simply coming from a dysfunctional family. It still astounds me that I remember even less of this novel than I assumed I would. And to think I was always so convinced Gordon wrote it and felt always that he was not honest with me in his response to my original claim of his authorship.

Chapter 32: An Image Mirrored in the Deep

How is it that Freddy hears himself think and we, in turn, get to listen to him? Something is not right inside his head. He hears voices. He sees Baby Ruth running naked through the sand dunes. He sees Jo-Jo watching her. The hair on Baby Ruth's head is golden, but curls black between her legs. Freddy is a child who has already witnessed too much. And still, the hurricane comes. The storm's eye is off the island of Jamaica. Freddy has a difficult time staying focussed. There is little to hope for in Freddy's life. And though this novel was published in 1971 it could have been written today. But all the crazy talk and sing-song chirping adds little to the dreadful consequences sure to come. It is a distraction. Liken it to a smoke screen, or a frightened little boy walking home alone in the dark. The nervous whistling never stops. Or the heavily-labored breathing resulting from Freddy's climbing and jumping over obstacles, made-up or crumbling. The possibility exists for an over-reaction, or a misread text or preconception. Might call it a prejudice. Or bigotry. And in many cases racist. Yesterday, on the spontaneous occasion of our first introduction to a northern neighbor who unfortunately lives too near to us at our cabin in Michigan, she surprisingly informed us there was *once even a black couple who lived across the street from her*, but they had since moved. She dowdily reported she used to work in an office with the lady, and added *the couple stayed for the most part quiet while living there.* And that, she mentioned on our leave, seemed good enough for her.

It is completely natural for any reader of *Sunshine* to turn presumptuous and resort to prejudicial feelings in cases where Freddy narrates as if his family and affairs are socially acceptable and of a particular norm. Though there are certainly families that exist in the world who share many of the same views as Freddy's family, it is unacceptable to be tolerant of them. And though sex is the driving force for most, nobody can claim with any certainty that our impulses and desires often get the best of us. Gordon Lish uses these sexual concepts as a constant theme in all his writings. Based on what Gordon has told me, he often practiced in his own life adulterous behavior when it came to his own sexual proclivities. According to his word and in his books, Gordon has always been unfaithful, having numerous lovers and rendezvous. For him, he always claimed, sex was the most important thing. From a very young age everything about him was ordered so, and arranged within the express purpose of acquiring a new lover, or conquest, or adventurous liaison, and it mattered little later in life who they were or even what they looked like. Several years ago my wife and I were having lunch with Gordon in a small Cuban restaurant on the corner of Broadway and Broome that he called *The Pork Store*. Rising rents a few years ago forced the restaurant to relocate. While we were sharing a meal together and visiting, a young woman approached our table inquiringly after overhearing something of our conversation. Surprised, I then observed Gordon attempt to seduce her, this young woman who wasn't at all attractive to my eyes, he suggesting she join him later at his apartment.

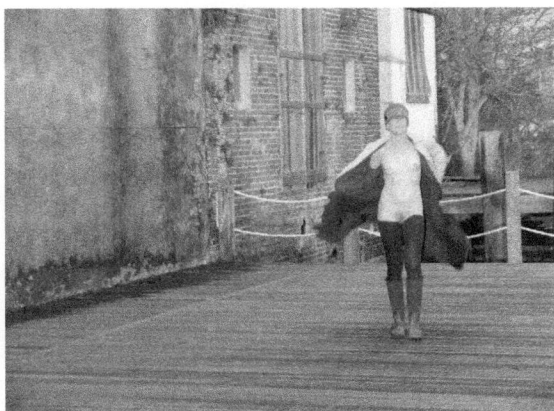

Chapter 33: The Usher and the King

In Freddy's household untoward events often occur simultaneously. If the words of Freddy, the narrator, are to be believed then the family's housekeeper Baby Ruth is sexually abusing him. According to young Freddy she runs around naked and grabs at his penis while chasing him. She asks him to put his fingers inside her private place. He tells us she is wet and hairy there. Baby Ruth, at times, plays with Freddy's *thing*. She puts it in her mouth and does *some sucking and moving up and down*. The family certainly appears to be deranged but functionally insane. Can there be any good that comes from their perverse behavior? Or by my reading of it somehow justify my own deviant thoughts? I admit that for years my erotic ideas have been entirely unclean. Sexual trysts imagined within the walls of my own home. So now I question whether it is possible that this type of behavior is actually more routine and acceptable than our social norms and attitudes would have us to believe. I have, from time to time, glanced up at second floor windows of a neighbor's home and wondered aloud to my wife what might be going on up there that we are unaware of? It is very hard to say. Often we read of our most conservative and Christian politicians turning out to be perverts, and those of us so adamantly opposed to unseemly sexual behavior seem to practice it ourselves. Experience has taught me that sexual deviance is more common than previously believed. Seems like anything goes among consenting adults. But this novel has the child narrator as its victim, or at least he is passive in his participation, and likely because what Baby Ruth does to him feels so good.

The contemporary French writer Marie Redonnet, in what seems to be blatant in every one of her small books, has her young female characters nonchalantly experiencing, for example, their first menstrual period, falling prey to lecherous men who only want to use them as sex objects, and the girls routinely coming back for more sexual abuse even from the same pathetic lechers. Never is there any love involved, nor emotion, only sex as if it was as normal and acceptable as the setting sun. Prostituting oneself is also expressed nonchalantly and assumed acceptable. It means nothing to these girls to be violently thrown onto their backs in the sand and taken, to be ordered to strip naked and be penetrated, or to be turned over and entered from behind. It is all presented in her text as indifferent, matter-of-fact, no despair, no feeling of injustice or their having been violated. Instead the young girls continue to expect more of the same, and even go looking for it. And it is disconcerting to realize there is rarely a decent man available in these books to ever have a caring and loving relationship with.

Chapter 34: It Seems We All Commit Adultery in Our Dreams

There are certain occasions when Hagen's work flies off its hinges, that a page becomes unglued. And possibly it is by design. Poop-pa, for example, suddenly is shown to have legs that are immobile and needing electric lifts to raise them. Other times he stands defiantly on his own and walks, appearing as an angry citizen milking the system and living on the dole. In contrast Freddy is portrayed as a young child growing up in a severely dysfunctional home. His brother dead, and their handyman shoving his *thing in her mouth* and her *tongue touching it.* And then without warning we find Freddy suddenly locked inside his mother's room as if she were also dead and gone, Freddy modeling all her clothes in the closet, applying her makeup in the mirror, finding a wig and attempting to walk in the same manner as she did. Insanely crazy events are happening in this wretched garden apocalypse of Florida. But there is no sunshine, and we continue to impatiently wait as the rain threatens to turn into hurricane winds and water. In fits and starts the literary action at times is fun, robust even, but oftentimes simply insane and exhausting. What seems normal in the text is that which can be related to as typical, everyday references, to our world. There is a connection to everything, precisely as Schopenhauer says there is. Common threads that bind us reach out at times to strangle us. They touch us as little else can.

According to Freddy, Baby Ruth pays him a dollar to smell between her legs. It would be amazingly difficult to prove this book is anything more than a writer's exercise in perversion. There is deviant behavior on almost every page. It is as if Clifford Hagen (or Gordon Lish) was preparing us for a thing by making perversion the norm rather than the exception.

Chapter 35: He Must See the Mutilated Crockery

Freddy's brother is dead and his mother has been sent to the hospital. Freddy insists on reacting to all of this with racially-soured outbursts while performing an absurd cruelty upstairs on a captured bird he named Jim Crow that he proceeds to drown in the now overflowing toilet. The entire household is in a state of crisis. The future does not bode well for any of them, and if there is any hope at all it would be for a continuance, if possible, of simply more of the same. It appears to be a pitiful existence for all who live in this environment. A futile life of one exigency after another. And in these small spaces boredom somehow continues to reign and hover like a black cloud over them, threatening a hurricane or unhealthy reactions to an already faithless life. Faithless in the sense of having nothing to look forward to but, for example, watching cartoons.

The entire book seems to be a projection of the great storm ahead. Already the detritus of poor lives have washed up on shore. Their beach encroached by littered remains. A perpetual wind and pouring rain. Crazy talk and obscene thoughts becoming the dialect of this region. A forgotten coast teeming with storms and wild birds, creatures emerging from the sea angered enough to eat us. A test for how much a person can endure. And in all this incessant and unceasing retort I wonder what the premise was for my thinking Gordon Lish may have written it?

I, perhaps erroneously, know in my heart that he did. But why? Was it the writing, or the person of Lish, who offered us up? All the many correspondences and hours spent in class listening to him teach had certainly affected my consciousness. But a touch of the unconscious is what I actually crave.

Chapter 36: *The Ravens of the Valley Shall Pluck Us*

Poop-pa is a crippled man and now I am too. When I fell from the roof of my Michigan cabin in 2010 my life was put on hold for six months. Like Poop-pa I was confined to a wheelchair. For that period I became a spectator of a life I had previously been rather physically engaged in. I had always performed the daily maintenance on our homes, made the repairs, and built by my own hand any additions and new buildings. That was what I was doing when I fell. Our cabin up north needed new paint. I was near the top of an extension ladder scraping the loose paint off the fascia, reaching and knowing I was stretching out too far, and I fell. Broke my leg in six places, shattering my right knee, dislocated my shoulder, and fractured my left arm. It took many months for me to heal. Then therapy and exercise, along with pain medication and time, and eventually I was good enough to walk without a cane. But never again would I be the same. It involves triple the time to accomplish anything. But at least I am no longer a spectator. The fall happened on an Easter Sunday which happens to also be the annual holiday of my last alcoholic drink back in 1986. These days I make it a point to remain seated in my chair on most Easter Sundays. Being a temporary invalid certainly changed me. The reality of now being a wounded animal made me think the entire infidelity my wife and I were conducting was more than a bit stupid to have even considered. I was so grateful we had not gone through with any of my sexual fantasies. As damaged as I was this potential cuckoldry would have made me feel emasculated. Incommensurate and defeated. All previous discussions regarding my wife conducting adulterous affairs now ceased and quickly lost their meaning. Life, and our marital relationship, seemed more brittle. And certainly less worth the potential risk of us doing irreparable harm to whatever might be left of it. Of course, in time, my position would soften and change. And what were possibly just crazy thoughts eased their way back in.

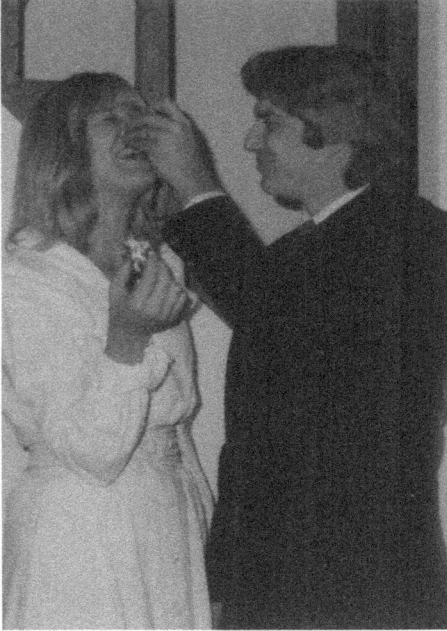

Freddy wants to exist where others cannot see him. There is no place in which to hide so well they cannot find him. A physical beating is perpetually threatened. His punishment promises to be severe. There is now an animal wildness about him. Freddy is uncaged, and stalking on high alert. His tattered old home rots within an encroaching culture of decay. Freddy will make a distinctively worn path from the beach back to his house. There seems nowhere else for him to go. His repetitive actions are set against a dramatic background, fast and furious in its constant insanity. A frightening world in which Freddy reluctantly abides along with Mr. Talking Frog, an amphibian always dressed distinctly in his white necktie.

Chapter 37: Nothing Happening Once is Real

The incessant repetition and rapid-fire crazy talk
ricocheting off Clifford Hagen's pen resembles in
some ways the speech of Gordon Lish in both his
fictions and in person. But Gordon is much more
sophisticated in his use of language. His
sentences are beautifully constructed and refined,
far superior to any of those produced in this book
by Clifford Hagen. Perhaps this is the reason
why Hagen was only a one-book wonder. But
how does a young unknown author first get the
attention of a major publishing house, have his
book published, and then disappear forever? It
does not make sense that there is no personal

history that follows behind him. Past, and even current reviews, of this book are rare, and available copies of the book limited to a few independent booksellers. What happened to all the remainder copies? Certainly this book did not sell out of its first run. There isn't even an ISBN number, which in 1971 almost all major publishers were using as a way to identify their product and have it catalogued. Gordon told me he could understand why I thought he might be the author, but did not elaborate. But I seriously note here that every character in this book is quirky and their dialogue reads as if they are insane. And there is never any sense of redemption to come, but instead only lives given over to complete despair crouched under a wobbling and tattered umbrella of dark, menacing clouds.

Freddy asks Baby Ruth if she loves Jo-Jo the way his mother did before she went away? Of course Baby Ruth acts surprised and wants to know herself what Freddy is talking about, as in how much does he know? But Freddy is never clear. He is simply a repeater of what he hears and sees. Not untypical in the dishonesty presented by most of us. Baby Ruth and Jo-Jo rarely, if ever, admit to anything. But Freddy knows, and though he may not fully grasp what it is his eyes and ears have provided him, he understands about the hairy place that smells and where sometimes people place their mouths inside. He also knows that something significant happens to his own *thing* when it is touched in a certain way. Love is a still a mystery to Freddy in all its different examples of expression, but he knows that love entails a personal touch, and often with no clothes on. There is a wild stench here, permeating every page.

There is small measure of anything clear regarding Freddy's family, except for a mutual insanity fed by their bickering meanness. Sobs heard coming from this awfully sad house on the Gulf would certainly fall on deaf ears or be ridiculed. Matters would certainly become worse the more one complained about them. Little consideration or kindness is afforded anybody. Needs are met at a minimum except as they pertain to sex. Animal desire and impulse are what matters most to these adults. Possibly our own decorum and civility shades this underlying fact hidden in all relationships. There is so much to be confused about the present tense due to faulty memories. We see Freddy taking scissors to a photograph in which he gives his mother a permanent smile for him to gaze upon within a wash of sunlight streaming from the window beside her bed. A frightened image presents itself to me as I imagine the contemporary Christian TV evangelist Joel Osteen, when he is eventually deceased, resting in his open casket with that permanent smile of his own that I perceive as not only surgically ridiculous but also quite hideous to the effect of being profoundly frightening.

Chapter 38: He Knelt at the Feet of Vain Women

Freddy anxiously awaits the return of his mother. Kept in the bughouse, or already buried in the deep blue sea, her return home is dubious, at best. But this reader, or any other, never sees this happen. One moment Mama is upstairs on her bed fucking Jo-Jo and by the next page she is gone. Perhaps it has to do with something left unsaid about her dead son and the grief that surely must have overcome her. This is a book made of *coming distractions in the midst of continued chaos*. A careful study, ripe with piercing dialogue, angry and racist in its tone, and my own predictable reaction to it all borders on bigotry itself and growing condescension. Little compassion can be expressed for these four remaining misfits. It feels as if my own lynch crowd is gathering, collecting rotten vegetables in which to have something to hurl at them. Page after page of disgusting anecdotes clattering on and on in their chirping repetitions daring me to stop listening. But in a recreational sense, even though the novel promises to eventually go nowhere, and offers no hope ever for any resolution, it is necessary to complete my assignment. And at its finality, I suppose I will have arrived at the doorpost of my suffering.

It must be overwhelming to be Freddy. Not knowing who you are, and waiting for a dysfunctional adult to eventually explain things in a way you might understand. Having to witness and be in the company of complete strangers up close attending a funeral wake within the walls of an unhappy home, outsiders speaking of a mysterious *better place* his dead brother went to, and so many visitors carefully whispering about his mother. All we are privy to at this stage of the novel is that his mother simply went away. Meanwhile, in another room, Poop-pa spins around on the wheels of his invalid chair, takes a moment to look into the mirror on the wall making believe he is Hitler, speaking his own version of German, and taking a comb to his hair. But there is nothing funny, or charming, about this family. Basically it consists of sadness and despair, with a bit of sexual perversion thrown in. Diversion deployed as a pressure release. It is only when certain truths are revealed that the house surely will come off its pilings. In theory, pilings driven so deep into the Gulf sand that even a hurricane might fail to lift it.

Suddenly, and with no warning nor any event leading up to the present crisis, Jo-Jo is seen standing in the blowing wind and rain outside the locked door, pleading with Freddy to please let him back in. But be forewarned, it is always a dead end to ever jump to your own conclusions in *Sunshine*. There is nothing sacred here, especially the truth. Except for all the crazy talk and constant chattering, there is nothing to suggest Gordon Lish wrote this unless we focus specifically on his own obsession with sex. For years I have recalled in my thinking that Lish wrote this book, my reasons being hinged on the incessant chatter and completely insane character of the book itself. But I did not remember all this sex so prevalent in it. Or the violence and frustration given over to a terrible master's dominion. Or the constant threat of a hurricane's coming destruction and the dreaded force of its gale winds. What I realize now is from beginning to end there is no paradise in Freddy's world. Something is coming for Freddy as well as a foreboding for me, and it is proving less promising now to discern what that something is.

Chapter 39: One False Note

Who can judge which character is worse? There are so many. Jo-Jo locked out of the house in the pouring rain, the window now broken by a vase crammed with plastic flowers. The hard rain pummeling, forcing itself inside, and nothing to do about it as the one person who might have fixed the sash has suddenly gone missing. Freddy being such a jerk of a kid who dismisses the drenched-man's overtures to let him back inside. Baby Ruth in her anger at this bad man she feels is now attempting to rape her as well, she who threw that pot of plastic flowers at him breaking the glass in the window that now lets the rain blow in. Obviously, none of these people are all that bright, and it seems doubtful that any of them are worth saving from this, or any, impending storm. Life on the Gulf, with these characters, is certainly no paradise. Baby Ruth and Poop-pa are both naked upstairs and rolling on the bed. Freddy looks on from his safe hiding place draped within the clothes closet. A scurrilous middle inning of a typical full game of foul play. Loud sex and noise downstairs coming from the TV and Mr. Talking Frog. Nothing else is missing. Except for Jo-Jo who is bound to eventually make his way back inside. Nothing can stop these characters of Hagen's from suiting up and returning to the scene of their obscene lives. The pregnant crashing of the sea remains deafening.

We are informed the name of the hospital is Avon Park. The intent of the staff is to make Mama well and then return her back home. Meanwhile, at the house she must come back to, Baby Ruth and Poop-pa are again having wild sex. Even with his limp and crippled legs wrapped around her head they manage to whip each other's behind with a leather belt while Poop-pa precisely aims his burning cigarette, singeing the hair between her legs. Baby Ruth is shown to be quite animated even with all that amazing blubber she carries, dangling disgustingly off her body. We also witness Poop-pa's wheelchair slamming repeatedly into the side of the bed, the cripple's arms grasping to lock onto her, as Baby Ruth scrambles to wrap her own sweaty thighs around Poop-pa's head. Nothing but insanity, exhibited in countless ways to prove and make believers out of the most skeptical ones among us. Clifford Hagen has written his text upon us, and has come to make us see a world of his making. Though his soiling of us is not yet complete, the stain is never to be washed away. Obviously a complete saturation was his mission and intention when he first sat down to write. His purpose for his everyday scribbling. A vastly important endeavor, as well, to the person wielding my pen. Poop-pa says that Mama's coming home. One more week and she will return to this crazy household they call home. Meanwhile Jo-Jo and Baby Ruth have taken off in the Ford to go shopping with Poop-pa's money. Freddy sits at home in front of a blank screen, opting to not turn the TV on. Poop-pa remarks to Freddy that Baby Ruth is a "real woman". Freddy certainly agrees with that assessment. A growing confidence continues to favor the odds of there never being a suitable resolution resulting in anything positive throughout the duration of this book. Even with such little hope remaining there seems for me a contentment with my feeling dissatisfied as I wallow in the stench and disgust of this pathetic human behavior. Sad to say, this is not a dated novel, but a story of our present time. And I still want to believe that Gordon Lish wrote it. It would help explain things. The very back of the book jacket features a photograph of Clifford Hagen who even resembles a younger Gordon Lish. The seated man is shown relaxing next to a large body of water that could certainly be the Gulf. There is a two sentence biographical statement under the photograph that says, "Clifford Hagen lives in Florida, where he was born in 1943. He likes girls, fishing, sports cars and bourbon, and only writes when he feels like it — which is most of the time."

CLIFFORD HAGEN lives in Florida, where he was born in 1943. He likes girls, fishing, sports cars and bourbon, and only writes when he feels like it—"which is most of the time."

I mailed Gordon the book so he could have a look at it. He mailed it back to me along with this letter.

Dear Mike,

No, I am not Clifford Hagen. I'm handsomer and a better writer, only except I also like girls, like fishing okay enough, can live without sports cars, but did drink bourbon when it was 1971. The other thing is I can see why you'd think I'm Clifford Hagen, but, honest, if I was, I would have

changed my name to read Hagan, not Hagen.
That's how much a better writer I am —and
handsomer speaks for itself.

All thanks for the read.

Gordon

Dear Mike,

No, I'm not Clifford Hagen. I'm handsomer and a better writer,
only except I also like girls, like fishing okay enough, can live
without sports cars, but did drink bourbon when it was 1971. The
other thing is I can see why you'd think I'm Clifford Hagen, but,
honest, if I was, I would have changed my name to read Hagan, not
Hagen. That's how much of a better writer I am--and handsomer
speaks for itself.

All thanks for the read.

Chapter 40: Upon a Whirling Landscape

Given the amount of hate and vitriol spewing
from every character in this Hagen-developed
household, it is interesting that the only silent one
among them has been Freddy's mother who has
yet to return home from the mental hospital. It is
possible she, by her own design, removed herself
from Poop-pa in order to escape all his
manufactured chaos and insanity. Almost as if
being aloft, or aloof, she deigns to keep her head
floating in the clouds. Certainly she must know
the idea of her returning home to this family will
be her death sentence. She would be much better

served by staying as far away as possible from this band of misfits and idiots. Today Jo-Jo asked Freddy to steal money from out of Baby Ruth's purse. Of course, Freddy already knows all of Baby Ruth's hiding places, but he no longer wishes to cooperate with and assist Jo-Jo. At least in the eyes of the household it seems Jo-Jo has turned bad. This is certainly a severe case of the pot calling the kettle black.

In one turn of the page certain roles are reversed. Poop-pa is walking around the kitchen table banging the surface with his hands, Mama is upset and screaming. Freddy is under the table watching adult legs scurrying about and circling while Jo-Jo is laid out on the floor, his back leaning against the brick wall of the fireplace, his legs roped together with tape stretched across his mouth. Poop-pa stops pacing enough to kick him once hard. Though logic has them all eventually killing each other, there is no contiguity for the resulting action. There is no sense, and nothing chronological. It seems Hagen merely sits down to compose a page, any page, and then throws it onto his dangling game board as if he is drunk and playing bar darts. There is no story, only incidents. The novel suggests that even boarded-up windows let the storms come in. That sheets of rain portend to drown us. It feels at this stage of my reading that nothing would satisfy Clifford Hagen more than to see every one of us readers dead as well. Page after page of despicable events including his scourge of crawling armies of sand crabs coming out of the sea to harm us. How appropriate it would be to bring closure to these pathetic lives. Nothing here is promising enough to ever be worth saving.

Of course, as expected, we learn two pages later that Mama is back home. And the reason that Jo-Jo is tied up to the fireplace and being kicked senseless is because Freddy told Poop-pa about him seeing Mama and Jo-Jo having sex on the bed. Mama claims the story is all "made-up". That Freddy, when left alone, has a vivid imagination. What concerns me now is how well Poop-pa gets along on his previously two dead legs. Well enough that he kicks Jo-Jo and circles the kitchen table endlessly. Mama insists the black man was only fixing the broken bedroom window. Poop-pa counters and contends that the black man was instead fucking her, got caught, and then attempted to escape out of the upstairs window. Mama pleads with her husband to leave the young child out of it, that he has no need to hear this rubbish talk being said about her and Jo-Jo. It is most difficult for a reader to know what to think. Our eyes and ears from the beginning have witnessed everything through Freddy, and intuitively we know he cannot be trusted either. Not only is Freddy obviously a mentally and emotionally disturbed child, he comes from a family teeming with the illness. It is a wonder how jealousy has any say at all as it seems everybody is getting penetrated by something or other. The nonsense is most stifling.

Chapter 41: No Longer Winter Winds

Freddy does have a memory of once having a normal family. A past when proper table service was appropriated and good meals prepared and enjoyed. When all hell is breaking loose Freddy goes back to that time in his mind. Events such as Poop-pa screaming and calling Freddy's mother a *whore*. And then, as fleeting as these once-comforting memories seem to be, we suddenly discover Mama lifeless, her body resting in the tub, the bath water red and still steaming. I know this novel will certainly not have a happy ending. Freddy will continue to venture even further into his world of fantasy and it is hoped Poop-pa is somehow justly crucified for his despicable behavior. Poop-pa seems to get along so well on his legs now that he can tie-up and torture the people he considers evil in his life. Poop-pa is a mean and angry man. The common thread throughout this household is that everyone is equally unhappy. Freddy is so frightened he scurries to hide under a chair or the table. He is lifted enough off the ground to be beaten, slapped across the face, and denied any sense of safety a good home might provide. His is a labyrinth prison, with no way out but the course his mother has already taken. Poop-pa is a dictator whose kingdom is in decline.

What little grasp Freddy seemed to have on reality has now been completely lost. There is so much confusion, anxiety, and disruption in this household that Freddy latches on to anything that might bring him some peace or semblance of stability. His memory of Aunt Eva and a Thanksgiving long ago, with Poop-pa in his wheelchair bellyaching like a baby, slapping his spoon on the table in a childish fit. And then everybody was supposed to be kind to Mama when she returned home from the hospital, but instead she lies there dead in a pool of blood, floating in the bathtub. Not even Mr. Talking Frog can possibly spare this disaster for Freddy. The only routine suggesting any sanity has symbolically washed away in the pouring rain. The players seem to all be waiting for their cue to act crazy again. And rather, because there is never an innocent dog to beat, a black man finds himself chained to the wall as the fat lady helper tends to the sexual needs of a purely despicable man. Clifford Hagen obviously has filled this novel with excrement and my bet is he intended all along to permeate these pages with its awful stench.

Flash back in time to the funeral box Freddy's brother rests in looking "deader than a doornail". Freddy standing attentively, up close to him, touching his cold face, his fingers feeling like the flowers of every color shrouding him. A capital mistake and ultimate confusion. Freddy, with his mother at his side, knowing that someday it will be himself blanketed by these flowers, dirt being thrown from above down onto his face. Clifford Hagen is probably dead himself by now. Or he is a crazy man wandering the back roads and alleys of a small town in Florida. Or skipping stones out into the Gulf of Mexico. Eating shrimp-on-a-stick and downing beer chasers. Or perhaps playing *Trivia* in The Tap Room surrounded by his drinking friends he might call acquaintances. It is a fact that people generally care only about matters concerning themselves. But these same people typically say they will pray for us and constantly remind us to *just have faith*, that *things will get better*. Driving rain pales in comparison to the vitriol that issues from the lips of Baby Ruth and Jo-Jo both trying to make a go of it in a sick and tired white man's world.

Chapter 42: Sad Dead Millions

Truth is if it weren't for my obsessiveness in attempting to figure out this fantasy of mine I would have quit reading this summer drivel several pages ago. This book is actually pretty stupid, as well as insane, and I have no clue as to why it was ever written, or even published. Who writes a crazy book like this, gets a major publisher interested in it, and then vanishes from the face of the earth? A man named Clifford Hagen is not the author of this book. But the trademark voice of the Gordon Lish I know is not present in it either. There are few words among the pages that make me think of Lish. Gordon loves to use words lyrically, poetically, and to make of something that isn't. The sex and rash behavior on the page is of course Lishian, or could be construed, mis or otherwise, to be his too. Sex plays an enormous role in Lish's life as well as in his work. For as long as I have known Gordon he has exhibited an insatiable hunger for anything having to do with sex. But I never once witnessed him as inappropriate or making an untoward advance toward any female anywhere. Several years ago my wife and I were strolling through SOHO with Gordon and he took us inside this wonderful grocery market filled with gourmet items he wanted us to see. Suddenly he noticed a man shopping in another aisle, off to his side, not far from us, and he hurriedly, almost frantically, gathered us to shepherd a fast exit from the store, frantically telling us as we were escaping that the man was a professor at NYU and Gordon had recently fucked his wife and the man knew about it. He was concerned the offended husband was perhaps stalking him so we all needed to remove ourselves quickly and as far away as possible from this tortured husband's vicinity.

Gordon Lish wrote a novel some years ago titled *Peru*. It is generally recognized as his masterpiece. I used to agree with that assessment, but have since changed my mind. The voice he used in that book does remind me somewhat of Freddy. Both narrators are speaking as adults as they relate episodes of their past, but they are as children in their storytelling. They speak as if they are still children. Both authors might have come from completely different backgrounds, but they share a common insanity in their voices. Gordon obviously writes from a more privileged upbringing than Hagen who figures to actually be a product of the Florida Gulf. *The Redneck Riviera* is the unflattering designation the Gulf has been branded with for quite some time. What is interesting to me is that black slaves, in that part of the country prior to the Civil War, were free and allowed to own property and have a life and property outside their required servitude. They could come and go as they pleased so there isn't the typical animosity today between the races in that part of the country that is prevalent in a city such as Louisville, Kentucky. In Louisville one is brutally aware of the palpable hard feelings that still persist and run deep within both cultures. But, even in this book *Sunshine*, supposedly taking place in the deep south, and particularly the Florida Gulf, there is still the dreadful taunting and calling of names. And the bulk of this racism comes from the lips of Freddy himself who regularly uses the word *nigger* to inflict his pain. He had to have learned it somewhere, and most likely from his father who still uses a black woman as if he owns her. Poop-pa carries an air of superiority over his black help, which makes little sense as he wheels himself around in his wheelchair barking orders he believes still matter. In reality he is a crippled old man nobody listens to.

Sunshine is a novel easily discounted and perhaps, if read, widely ridiculed. Gordon Lish has more readers than Clifford Hagen, though none of Lish's books have ever gone into a second printing, and all of them are eventually remaindered and all go out-of-print. Every few years a publisher will reprint, or reissue, the works of Gordon Lish in order to keep him in print or perhaps in some way make a name for themselves by hanging on his coattails. But the fact remains that all of Lish's titles are available to purchase for a few cents on the dollar and with new editions being published there will be even more inexpensive copies made available than ever before. If Lish ever does get the attention he rightfully deserves for his writing it would be preferable that his out-of-print works become collectible, and thus more desirable to readers. The reading public would actually demand then an affordable printing because they actually want to read him. Lish, along with his publishers, has supersaturated the marketplace and made himself even more disowned by the literary types who might have raised him from the ashes of his own doing. It is better to die on the vine than to continue harvesting fruit nobody is interested in consuming.

Chapter 43: Abroad with Painted Lips

Though the most delightful and entertaining travelogue I have ever read, the last section of *Travels with Charley* by John Steinbeck, for me, turned quite disturbing. Steinbeck used the last section as his platform to present his personal views on racism in the United States from his time of growing up in Salinas, California in the early 1900's through the present day described as happening in 1960 in New Orleans. There, a group of forty women calling themselves *The Cheerleaders* stood outside an elementary school chanting racial slurs at the young black children making their way to, and from, their classrooms. Steinbeck himself witnessed first-hand the crowds gathered to watch this spectacle and who unapologetically applauded these cheerleaders and their performances. The book made me look at my own experience with people of color and I realized, finally, that I was not one of these vile racists with hatred in my heart and head for people different than myself. All throughout the day after finishing my reading of the book I examined my present and historical feelings regarding the civil rights movement, mixed-race relationships, and even the characters in this book *Sunshine* who spew so much anger and hatred it becomes sickening. I wondered if all the sex going on in this Hagen-made household was done out of spite and hatred for one another? Why this assumed act of love was used as a weapon raised against the races is beyond my understanding.

Chapter 44: A Bell, a Tree, a Leaf, a Cloud

There is the constant pull and collaboration of twos:...There are parallel existences in nature, two sides to every story... life is never one-sided, is rarely straightforward, is connected to the past and the future. To exist is to speculate

circuitously, to wander and absorb sensation, and
to pause for the occasional ethereal
*aside.___*Fatima Shaik, *Miss MacIntosh, My*
Darling: Poetry of the Subconscious

Baby Ruth demands to be paid in cash on a
Sunday night, for the wages she has earned
laboring for Poop-pa and family. Of course,
Poop-pa has no money, no cash anyway, so Baby
Ruth has to settle for a check she cannot cash that
day or spend that coming evening. And as the
story goes, another simple blow to another typical
act, destined to result in smithereens. There will
never be any resolution to anything, and things
remain in a constant state of turmoil. I do wish
these stories were different. I want revelations.
The text was supposed to provide ample
opportunity to discover not only why I believed
Lish to be the author of this novel but also why I
came to love this man so much. For all my
gratitude I had nothing else to give of myself for
him but my writing. And I knew how much he
obsessed over sex and the elaborate theater and
dramatic affair of fucking all night. It was a
creative event for Gordon Lish, and something he
claimed to take quite seriously. He also kept a
scorecard, and he numbered his concubines in
levels of mutual satisfaction, motivated by results
and repeat performances, often lasting into the
wee hours of the morning. I believed my wife
would gratify him to such a degree that he would
appreciate my gift to him as much as I did, and
do, appreciate her myself.

Regarding the sexual collaboration between my

wife and I, and to us having two sides as in a *parallel existence in nature*, it has been widely reported that the positive experience sought through sexual arousal has several stages and may not lead to any actual sexual activity beyond a mental arousal and the physiological changes that accompany it. Typically, given sufficient sexual stimulation, sexual arousal in humans reaches its climax during an orgasm. But it may also be pursued for its own sake, even in the absence of an orgasm.

Chapter 45: A Time to Every Purpose Under Heaven

To learn about a person, to become intimate through reading biographies, actually falls short of being in that person's presence. The impossibility of relationships involving an introduction obviously rests solely on if they are dead. Encounters with historical icons through reading books is hardly the same as being present with them in the flesh. Collected letters involving their previous correspondences project more a promising truth on any path seeking familiarity. It is through these candid personal missives that authenticity might be revealed. I not only knew Gordon Lish personally, but we exchanged letters often. Some of our conversations and voice messages left via the landline telephone have also been recorded.

It is difficult to imagine how or when it began for

me, this obsession with a man of literature, an editor who I hoped might save me from myself and what I had become. In 1986, one year prior to my initial correspondence with him, I had quit drinking for good, my wife had left me, and I was separated from my youngest son. Of course all that changed in time. My wife came back, as did the emotional and financial responsibilities of fatherhood. But here I was, face down on our bed, the middle of a sunny day, the rays streaming warm through the second-floor bedroom window. I had just been notified that my cousin, whom I had grown up with, had died suddenly in a car wreck back home in Michigan. The booze and cocaine had finally gotten to him, that and a love lost but continually sought after. As I inappropriately sobbed and wailed face down on the bed I soon felt the presence of a comforting soul. To my surprise it was the man I had known in the many representations of Jesus found in my Lutheran hymnals and Sunday School literature. Ludicrously, and always, he resembled a white man with flowing hair and beard. And here at my bedside, perceived in the flesh, was the same man standing next to me. As real as any fantasy come true. But no prayer was ever answered, only His acceptance given to me, embraced through my personal suffering. This heavenly visitor, later to be explained away as simply my mind at work in strange and mysterious ways, its wonders to behold. One can imagine anything, and make true its benevolence. But I do believe it was this very day when I actually made the serious decision to follow the teachings of Gordon Lish. To learn how to discriminately read and become a

great writer. To eventually come to understand
his encrypted messages and become his friend.
And my wife would take this journey with me,
and we would together have a life teeming with
possibility and good favor. That was the dream I
truly wished that day to make a reality.

Chapter 46: Wading with the Ghost Crab

We learn that Baby Ruth is paid by check for the
entire month, and then she asks for three
additional days off per week to add to the two she

has off already. That makes five days total, which means she wants to only work two days per week, leaving Poop-pa alone in his wheelchair to care for Freddy who sits in front of the gray screen of his TV and watches Mr. Talking Frog. It appears to be a pretty good deal for Baby Ruth. But if Poop-pa could have risen up on those crippled legs of his he would have chased that woman down and beat her silly. And her demand for these extra liberties came immediately after he paid her for the entire month in advance. Baby Ruth does eventually settle for four days off on Poop-pa's condition she comes to work on Saturdays. There are not enough pages left in this slim novel for Hagen to construct the appropriate justice deserved for all these characters. I am wishful that perhaps the hurricane will blow them all away, or drown them. My memory unfortunately fails to provide me an ending that I can remember from my first reading so many years ago.

The story remains a platform for Hagen's anger and resentment. Confusion becomes the norm for young Freddy. It is impossible for him to make sense of all these events and it is through this composition that the reader understands this. A body cannot resist Hagen's charms. It is as if a witch doctor has placed a great curse upon us. Now we are all complicit in this insanity. Poop-pa sits in his wheelchair tending the smoldering wood and attempts to stoke a flame in the fireplace. The iron poker rests across his lap and portends to do great harm to anything venturing beyond the damp smoking logs. And Jo-Jo knows this, as does Freddy who keeps himself scarce under the table, hidden from the cruel eyes of his crippled father. Baby Ruth has stolen the Ford and driven off to Tampa even though it is understood she cannot drive. She told Jo-Jo she was going to visit her mother. Poop-pa waits for her return, and insists upon it. Jo-Jo is not so sure. Meanwhile smoke gathers under the mantle and the firewood smolders and refuses to ignite. There is little promise for any flame.

Chapter 47: Young Flesh is a Party

The blurb on the dust jacket claims Freddy's mind is "circular". He is insane. Or perhaps an extremely confused little boy. In that analysis, if true, Clifford Hagen succeeds. Within a couple of days I will have read this book for the second time over the course of twenty years. This title has, strangely enough, for two decades now, continued to beckon me from its place upon my shelf. A fitting call for closure and resolution to what has happened in my relationship with Gordon Lish. Just as words are incestual in the best-written works, so might our lives be as well. And perhaps analogous to me sprouting an elaborate fantasy that promises happiness for everybody. Segments coming together and staying put that way. But there is always some absent cog in the wheel. Numerous accounts have been written of incidents when Gordon Lish has been in social situations face to face with a writer he has worked extensively with and championed, and suddenly he asks him or her, "Do I know you?" This disremembering is devastating to the writer who has worked so hard to please Lish enough to get a book completed worthy of its getting into print. I would imagine these disavowed writers number over a hundred. Gordon often discounted to me writers he had worked with after they left him to publish on their own without his help. Of course, I myself have lately done the same. Still, I remain a steadfast friend to him and continue to acknowledge Gordon in all my dedications. It does seem to me that lately he has used what I believe, perhaps erroneously, to be a feigned sickness to avoid speaking to me. It may also simply be my imagination.

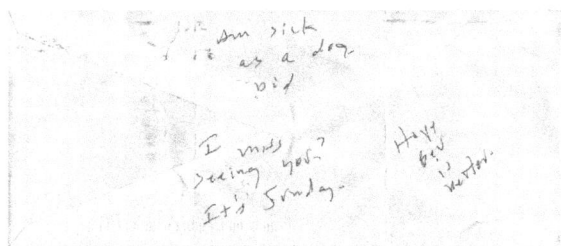

Chapter 48: The Folded Clock

Recently I have been exposed to the writing of another somewhat contemporary literary icon. Her name is Heidi Julavits, significant other to writer Ben Marcus who is an unconfirmed ex-student of infamous teacher, editor, and writer

Gordon Lish. I remember Gordon making some not-so-nice remarks to me about Ben Marcus due to his feeling slighted or unappreciated by him. Lish not feeling credited enough with helping him, or something or other to that effect. It happens a lot with The Teacher. But I am careful, always, to not let it happen with me. Or any perceived affronts to surface in any way. I respect his eccentricities with all its plagues and bouts of insecurity.

Heidi Julavits is one of the co-editors of the acclaimed magazine *The Believer* originating in San Francisco. She is also the author of several works previously ignored or unknown to me. But no longer is she kept at arm's length as I recently discovered her previously published diary *The Folded Clock*. What a delight to unearth this rare gem amidst these current days of our horrendous electorate deciding the outcome for president of these United States. Clearly a choice for POTUS between a highly qualified and rational woman and the unseemly, almost unbelievable, monstrous caricature going by the name of Donald Trump. Any literary diversion for me today is abundantly welcomed if it helps me escape my current nightmare in facing the truth about the worrisome state of our country. But note here as well that I have no fear of reprisal from any so-called Clinton-deemed *deplorable* as they are not of the stripe that reads my kind of drivel found on the sort of pages you are presently reading. I am also confident I could publish anything I want and face no immediate jeopardy in being found out by my few friends, even by my parents, or almost any other family member to speak of, less those I still remain in contact with. Numbers I must confess are few, and routinely dwindling.

A woman whose private thoughts had been for years confined to her journal, Julavits has wantonly written herself upon me. And in this somewhat substantial work Heidi Julavits details the many facts and facets of her daily life, her foibles and her prejudices, fairly and in a properly-sounding honesty rarely witnessed on the page. And respectfully, in frank contrast, I have never been able to connect with anything her husband has to say. Though I believe Ben Marcus is of much greater literary fame, I am incapable of understanding him, or perhaps the coded-ness of his words excludes me and bars me from entering the locked gates of his elitist club. It seems to happen more often to me with men. It is why I prefer to hang out (at least virtually) with women. But it is possible that I have never really applied myself to exercise an appropriate *try* in my entering the world as exampled in his first book *The Age of Wire and String*. But his wife Heidi is different. I get her. And I wish *my* own wife would read her book and get to know her as well. Good writing does that. But these two women certainly have to be completely different from each other, and not surprisingly, often the same. Except my wife is yet to know this herself. For years neither my wife nor I had any idea there were actually women in the world like Heidi Julavits. It is so refreshing to witness such honesty on the page. But of course Heidi might be lying and me, being the too-reclusive and naive dumb ass I have historically been, falling for Julavits like a delusional lonely patron visiting his first strip club. (Fact: No stripper is really in love with you. You just think she is. It is her job.)

Although her book is called a diary, in many ways it isn't. The individual episodes feel more like short essays to me. Each entry certainly does have a date on them just as diaries do, but they just as well could have been called chapters with titles heading them. The subjects vary widely, and are vast and numerous, but they always circle back to the personal Heidi Julavits and where she locates herself in each event, predicament, example, or given date. Unfortunately for us she doesn't drop important names, and that is understandable, and in good taste. But she does mention by name famous dead people. Few names, it seems, if they are still living. Sort of puts the whammy on getting the full picture unless the reader is as well-read and educated as Heidi obviously is. I believe her work fails in this respect. In my mind any celebrity, dead or alive, qualifies to have their name revealed for obvious reasons. Especially reclusive writers who have made a sizable income from their public works. And I noticed she even resisted mentioning the title of an Austrian Haneke movie she was using as prop in one of her chapters, and for me it seemed important enough to name the horrific *Funny Games* as substantive to her point. I do not get her reasoning behind making certain books and films a mystery the reader is required to already know of, or have need themselves to resort to Googling on the internet. But this is a small fault when measured against such a momentous and original example of fine writing.

Some critics of Heidi Julavits take issue with her perceived life of privilege. Having a successful husband and two young children, all of them living in New York City most of the year, the family spending three months of every glorious summer at their seasonal home in Maine, and traveling all over the world to places like Italy to attend artist's colonies and such, is certainly enviable, but she has earned it. I can only imagine all the hard work of her humble beginnings, the demands of networking in a most competitive environment, her participation in literary readings and symposiums, teaching and publishing, and her attempts at maintaining some semblance of a normal life while raising a family. Julavits appears to have no pretensions over believing she should win an award for being the best wife or mother. Like many of us she does the best she can.

Julavits says she reads with a fountain pen in her hand so she can fool herself into thinking she is writing. I prefer reading near my computer, if possible, as I often record notes and ideas that come to me in bursts. Too many times I am not in the vicinity of my handy keyboard with no pen nor paper in sight, and by the time I make it to either one I have forgotten the supposedly brilliant line I had just composed in my erratically winsome mind. It happened again this morning on my patio. I was remembering the very start of my reading this book on November 7, 2016, the unnerving fright-filled day before our POTUS election. And as I write this entry today the date is now November 13, a Sunday, and I only have a depressing (for me) nine pages left to read of *The Folded Clock* and I really do hate for this experience to end. But I also have come to better grips with myself over my candidate's loss. God, am I ever sick of politics, pundits, and tweets. Let's face it, the wrong person won, but we must get over it. Maybe he will somehow try to be a better person than he promised his *deplorables* he would be. And though I am exhibiting a rare tolerance for certain things Trump, my parents will not be given the same courtesy. I have yet to forgive them for reelecting Little George and The Dick to a disastrous second term in 2004. And they will receive no congratulatory call from me regarding their winning-candidate.

Yesterday I received by post two of the next three books I plan to read by Heidi Julavits, all novels, and surely to be in some measure disappointments for me. I cannot imagine her fiction possibly equaling the breadth and interest I felt in reading her diary. But what am I to do? Julavits says she has always wanted to be a novelist. But what if Julavits really knew how good she was with prose? I, for one, want more personal missives from her. She has so much to say, and I love how she says it. Such an engaging and fascinating personality comes through in her writing. Julavits always leaves me wanting. And desire, in all its many elaborate aberrations, is really never such a bad thing, is it?

Chapter 49: No Oozy Locks It Laves

The wife is the key, and the husband is the door
which will not close, and there is no such thing as
a new love in an old house, and there is no use
barking at the wind, the wave, the shadows.___
Marguerite Young, *Miss MacIntosh, My Darling.*

I want to know what became of Mama. All that
remains for us now is this vision of Mama and
Jo-Jo together naked on the bed upstairs and then
the black man flying out the window. And how
does a novel come to this? Or Baby Ruth,
de-robed on the beach, standing across from the
crippled Poop-pa in his chair, spreading out the
folds of her hairy vagina, shoving it into his face
and then pissing on him? Freddy standing in
wonder at what he is witnessing. Jo-Jo off to the
side taunting the young boy, harping that his
mother is dead. Freddy hoping for that hurricane

to actually come and destroy them. While reading this tiresome text my mind wanders, and I find myself thinking, *but at least it isn't as cold in Florida as it gets here at my cabin in Michigan.* The winds coming off the great Lake Huron are fierce and frigid. Especially after the nasty winter of last year. The ice well over four feet thick and not exiting the surface until well into spring.

Chapter 50: Swimming Behind a Wall of Water

Freddy brings his story to a close with Poop-pa leaning back into his chair, fingering the poker in front of the fireplace, and telling Freddy that he *knows*. After all the insanity and lack of good and gentle care for anybody, Poop-pa declares that, yes, *God is love.* And from that point on Freddy says he cannot remember another damn thing to relate to us *no matter how hard he tries.* And that is simply not good enough for me. I question what possessed this publishing house to proceed with the publication of this book? Was it pressure coming from the infamous Gordon Lish? Was he somehow involved in acquiring this novel for the publishing house, or perhaps in fact, he being the one who actually wrote it? It is impossible to say. But it is certainly not beyond my realm of thinking for him to have done such a thing. And if it was, it was not the last crappy book Lish ever had published. There have been many. So many, in fact, that I haven't even read them all. And some of these published works are even claimed by Lish himself to be amazing examples of contemporary fiction. And this is where we disagree sometimes in matters of important fiction. Gordon Lish, by his own admission, resists reading anything in translation. I have, at times for example, directed him to a foreign author I have discovered, who is far better than anything available to us in its original English, and he scoffs at my claims. But I do know he reads translations of his own choosing such as works by Thomas Bernhard, Julia Kristeva, and Gilles Deleuze, to name only three. And he pilfers quotes from all of them, using their foreign words that have been translated into English. And sometimes he even uses these little snippets of translation as introductions for the opening pages of his books. Fantastic literature is available to us in translation, and in numbers so amazing to me that I question why serious readers continue to read the drivel that they are being directed to in this country. It goes to prove how powerful marketing is and how much the herd wants to believe in anything it can.

Sunshine relates to us of a time and place of no
return. Whether it was the iron poker to his head,
or the traumatic experiences of losing his mother
and brother to tragic incidents, Freddy admits
failing to remember anything now beyond that
last page. It is quite possible, just as Holden
Caulfield did in *The Catcher in the Rye*, that
Freddy is writing this book from the confines of
his room in the same mental hospital his mother
had previously been admitted to. He says he is
trying hard to remember what came next, but to
no avail. Now everyone is pathetically stuck in a
limbo of Freddy's own making. But it wasn't as
if anyone was going anywhere anyway. The
perfect soiling of every despicable shred of
undergarment is gathered in a pile on the beach of
this coastal community. In this book there are
only Florida clouds, rain, and cascading tears.
This is certainly a novel easily discounted for its
literary value, same as are other books not so
easily understood. But if there is a hidden
message among these pages it would behoove us
all for it to come forth and be recognized. But it
is doubtful this final act of *Sunshine* will be
revealed, just as any clues to Hagen's truth will
undoubtedly remain forever *classified*. Clifford
Hagen will remain *a nobody* and Freddy will have
forgotten the rest of his life story. Hagen claims
on the back side of the dust jacket that he "*writes
all the time.*" That is, when he isn't "*chasing
pretty girls*" or "*driving fast cars*" while
"*drinking bourbon*". But unless he is dead he
cannot be forever young. And my guess is by
now, for his last act, he himself wanders the

streets woefully befuddled.

Chapter 51: Fly Your Skirt Upon Some Lonely Mountaintop

Gordon Lish, the teacher, *always* engaged in coquetry and made it no secret regarding his desire for sexual trysts outside of class. In his classroom all students were instructed, and required, to seduce him with their writing. He clearly stated this and scenes often rehearsed and presented in his lectures. Gordon insisted there be jeopardy always present on the page. Discreet remarks were also made, but nonetheless discouraged within a work of art. Where the legend stitches itself thin is in the gradual denial by Lish in current interviews for what is already known and now made consensus. For example, claims made as to whom he had previously bedded. And there were few, by his own claims, who could escape his charms if he was simply given a chance for a brief introduction. Enlarging further upon his reputation as a lady's man was one of his most serious vocations. When the teaching was finished and he had retired, for the first time in 1997, he announced to me that *fucking* would be his new art form. His focus on this latest enterprise became singular, and intense, as teaching and authoring had run their course and were no longer of viable worth to him. An evolution from within might have occurred as the natural course of events for a man now entering his eighties. But obviously it did not, and instead quickened itself into a medicated genius practicing his obsession with a predictably newly-avowed perversion.

Chapter 52: The Phantom of a Dead Love

Sunshine is a pathetic story about victims, Freddy being the most obvious one. But really, all of them are. The only way out of their dilemma is through death. Mama and baby brother chose that method. Freddy doesn't even trust the minister who conducts funerals in order for loved ones to supposedly get into heaven. In the mind of Freddy the actual purpose of a preacher is to eventually get somebody into a hole in the ground so he can throw dirt and flowers on him. It is discomfiting to Freddy that the preacher comes off as a bit of a prick. He, or Hagen's negative feelings about religion, may have been the motivation for all the graphic sex occurring in this book, the nudity, and poignant smells emanating from every orifice. Or the graphic literary display of Baby Ruth's legs splayed spread-eagle over the lips of the crippled Poop-pa laid flat-out on his back. Obviously Freddy's father Poop-pa does nothing admirable or redeemable but instead encourages every bad behavior. He operates his wheelchair recklessly and crashes into things. He carries an iron poker around on his lap looking to destroy something. Each page is another measure of how terrible and depressing a life can be. It is not unlikely that one day we might be faced, rather than simply fearing, a world full of people like Freddy. And all of them purportedly hunting crabs with their special homemade sticks as they go about their violent tasks wishing for their very own bicycle.

This Florida family seems oblivious to anything but this unending wet pour and their futile attempts at keeping water from ponding in the house. Today, as well, it is raining at my cabin here in the north woods of Michigan. The rain has a steady murmur to it. A droning rhythm as in this novel. And a nonsense rising daily in intensity. Violence has become for these people a natural and residing agenda in their everyday life. The despicable amazement of it all witnessed through their babbling expressions. It is their personal journey into the truth of all things, a derangement patterned on hanging onto another of their hopeless endeavors. It is never difficult to picture these characters in *Sunshine*. But we are kept at a distance from their faces. We hear the words coming from their mouths but fail to see their sad lips move or the frowns they must engage. And perhaps, in the end, Freddy, in his insanity, does indeed murder them all. And maybe Freddy was actually responsible for his brother's earlier death as well as his mother's. It goes to reason that these results would necessarily now be buried deep within his diseased and compartmentalized mind. It is also not hard to picture Freddy being kept inside a padded room in a hospital for the criminally insane. Freddy has attempted to claw himself back into his mother's womb, and is somewhat better for it.

Chapter 53: Our Natural Oblivion

"*... To be a writer is to assert yourself at the expense of others.*"___Gabriel Josipovici, *Writing and the Body*

After going along somewhat happily all through my younger years, as I look back on that time, I realize that I began to change as we are all wont to do. I sat myself down to read books daily and began to look for better answers to my life, searching for a truth that I felt was somehow escaping me. Something was definitely missing and I knew life had to mean more to me than what it had previously seemed to. And for years I established this diligent literary study, ultimately to no avail. I came to believe that life presented only questions, and the best authors were those who framed them most brilliantly and asked most succinctly for the reader's participation. Writers unafraid to broach their subjects honestly and with the best intentions. Today, it is deploring for me to read a book that is meant to only further a personal or social agenda, or to politicize an idea. But the individual standing up against the world, risking all in the spirit of principle, is another matter. Thomas Bernhard is the writer who comes to mind initially as *someone* whose rants are so refreshing and invigorating even within the harping of his consistently overwhelming repetitions. Bernhard is relentless in his attacks on the status quo. I cannot recall an instance when I disagreed with one of his diatribes or wished for him to stop all his complaining. It is as if he thinks nobody is listening to a word he has spoken and thus refuses to relinquish his battering offense. The writing of Gordon Lish is often compared to Thomas Bernhard due mostly to his own use of repetition. Clifford Hagen, though enough a comparable parrot, is nonetheless found lacking.

Chapter 54: Finding a Personality to Live With

*...It's that what's-the-use, born of the lower
vantage-ground and the closing-in shadows, that
chiefly makes me lonely — lonely to a
desperateness and on through a ruinous
calm.___Mary MacLane from I, Mary MacLane*

There are no cameras on the beach showing us
Freddy murdering sand crabs. Or his spiked stick
glistening with the wetness of fresh-killed flesh.
The meat blistering between fragments of hard
shells, broken, with gaping holes in them, their
liquids draining back into the sea. And the boy
never smiles. He is a determined chap and very
serious about what occupies his interest. He goes
about his killing with great passion. A serious
labor and profoundly intense. Nothing seems to
wear this boy out. Freddy is not normal and his

family members are most definitely kooks. His mother is married to a raging lunatic in a wheelchair, crippled and carrying an iron poker in his lap. And though disabled, still threatening vicious strikes and damage to anything that moves. Poop-pa tends a smoldering fireplace in the middle of hurricane season. He crashes that iron poker down, dismantling any serenity that might occasionally be present in the house. He violently fucks his female helper Baby Ruth as if he has every right to. And he does it in front of Freddy whose dead brother is never spoken of by name. A child gone and buried, with no explanation given. Freddy takes aim with his spear and hunts down his encroaching enemies. Freddy intends to end these lives through a vast, and thorough, annihilation.

Memories should not be trusted, nor ignored. The memories that do remain vivid to me are those I know I will never forget. They all seem to have been somewhat momentous occurrences. Extreme feelings of wonder, joy, fear, adventure, sadness, all of them present in whatever I have retained in my memory. Even exciting fantasies and experiments that were not followed through remain with me as if I had imagined myself doing them yesterday. The level of risk involved in these fantasies seems to play a huge role in what is ultimately remembered. An uncertain outcome that might have lead to some dire consequence is always at the forefront of my consciousness. But now, these years have seemed to have passed me by. All my sins of omission tend to hawk their specialties at me, taunting me for my historically chicken-like behavior.

Some days it feels as if the years pass you by and
suddenly you wake up sixty years old. But it may
instead be philosophically true that it is rather we
who pass, and time instead that actually stands
still. Nothing can prepare you for the realization
that you have already had your chance at life and
missed it. No matter how hard you have tried to
make of yourself something memorable and
concrete there is only the wild fandango left to
mollify. Every preparation engaged in creating
something results in a decimation of its
properties. Everything, always, returns to dust.
But my opulent life of sexual fantasy must remain
memorable, and to some degree because of the
robust threads of honesty built within this tale
which will most likely always remain a sort of
fiction. But there was certainly a coupling among
these dangerous ideas for romance. Ours has
been a marriage of long accomplishment, of
honor, and a lasting belief in the goodness of each
other. Attractions by, and for, the opposite sex
cannot be helped while coexisting in this animal
kingdom. There is no cleansing of a nest that can
get the stains of a life washed out of them. Even
those who claim they do not care make of life a
complication. Deceit, and the happy face some
people put on things, are enough to make you
want to shrink away from these horrid creatures.
Sometimes it is good to touch the forbidden
merchandise even though we have been ordered
not to do so. And there are times when perhaps
others should have a taste of what has been for

years graciously given for another to enjoy. I
certainly blame no man for ever wanting to. It
would be unnatural to suppress this desire, though
society has deemed these instruments materials
that destroy.

Chapter 55: The Veilings and Partings of Light

It has been several years since I first read
Sunshine, and that initial adventure seems
undependable in my present research. The fact is,
there is not one thing I remember about that first
reading except the dust jacket and Gordon's letter
to me stating that he wasn't the one who wrote it.
But he did say that he could see why I thought he
might have. He went on to say he is also much

better looking than Clifford Hagen, and if Hagen was the name he would be using he would have changed the spelling to read *Hagan.* Gordon also informed me that he never really liked to drive *hot cars* so much, but he did like *bourbon, and girls, and writing.* But none of that told me much about the supposed real author. Something was seriously wrong. The man himself, the personage, is missing in the history of Clifford Hagen, and the fellow who insisted he *writes all the time* has left no remains and nothing to prove his truth to us.

This writing exercise has already proven unreliable in the spirit of my always having something bearing down on my heart, demanding my acknowledgement of it, and expressing a penciled performance of some kind on the page. In ways, it can be likened to *writing on demand,* of which I do not do. My scribbling remains for me a supreme case of *as if,* just as Christopher Hitchens suggests. For a writer there is always the audience, but an assemblage not necessarily important enough that the text become mediated. There is no intimacy involved in this virtual world of readers who may never exist or even number beyond two. I hold no pretensions ever that my writing will be read, or least of all loved. But *I* love it or I would not perform these private acts on a daily basis. Nobody hovers behind me looking over my shoulder, examining every mark I might make on the page. What I am accomplishing in this exercise is simply a *warmup.* And by beginning each day with a new paragraph it becomes possible, within a slim chance, that an artifact of some worth shall come forth and surface from out of the depths of my unconscious. Perhaps a ritual better left to more gifted craftsmen, or a certain *liar for the ages,* a manipulator of time and movements to conjure. As previously mentioned, my general thoughts are typically filled with sexual fantasy, followed by despair. Ultimately, nothing ever works out for me as imagined. Non-teleologically speaking *it is what it is.*

Rarely do I discuss my own creative work with anyone. It is simply impossible to explain, and given my historical feelings of inadequacy, I fear never to be accepted or appreciated for my efforts whether on the page, through brush or pen, film, or photography. The truth is, throughout my life I have never fit in. And I quit trying to years ago. Even with the anointment by Gordon Lish recognizing and encouraging my poetic genius, I have never actively marketed myself among my peers or social media. And I remain hidden down here in Florida, safely protected by shadows and foliage. This does not mean I feel content with my standing in the art world. In contrast, I feel the extreme opposite. I seriously invest myself in search of great art whether it be still or moving pictures, painting, or language. My own work pleases me and I wonder, in a state of bewilderment, often why others who matter in literature have not discovered me. I feel I am one of the truly gifted artists among us. But I hold no pretensions that I will be acknowledged as such by my peers. Throughout my life I have never been lauded over anything. I somehow have failed to ever exist and can therefore never be forgotten. My work continues unimpeded and especially now in my later years absent any mediation. I create what I am impelled to make for no other reason than to give my own life meaning and derive some satisfaction from putting in a good day's work. I write "as if" and expect it to be so one day. There is nothing today in my physical appearance or performance that might draw the masses to me. Unlike Bob Dylan or Patti Smith, performance art eludes me. There will be no attention garnered by my singing or my dance, only the presence of silence in these words and pictures I make on the page. But my work awaits a coarse enactment within the reader's blood and brains.

...Being a changeling child is torment, as the child never quite understands why acceptance is being withheld, but for an adult, being beholden to no one is a thrilling little terror. ___The Dead Ladies Project by Jessa Crispin

Chapter 56: He with the Flaming Hair

All this study and still no answers. The main player in all this might as well be dead. Hagen, Lish? It is all the same to me. Too many similarities to list, but no disclosures to report. In a fiction-writing class in Bloomington, Indiana Gordon once announced to the class that in his mind there is always a giant billboard beside the road at the entrance to the mall parking lot advertising, *Everything for Gordon!* He is serious, and I can even imagine him as a child stomping his feet in protest over what he felt was being kept away from him and instead rightfully his. Gordon's rules for the road. I am forever impressed by the dashing figure he cut in the author's photograph on the back of the book jacket of *What I Know So Far*. I believe Gordon when he claims he is quite the lady's man. This seems to be the most important thing he feels he has to prove. And, most likely, his extremely competitive nature plays an enormous role in many of his personal and business failings. Or his having to be in control of every situation no matter the consequences.

ISBN 0-03-070609-2
Ref:0584:001445:50

Chapter 57: A Diminishing Return

A strong-willed creator lends himself far less to collective influence than a merely talented artist, whose work may easily be made the material for a mass creation that genius opposes. ___Otto Rank from Art and Artist

A writer's mark on the page does not immediately make it genius. Better to exasperate one's sentences. Make them worthwhile to the person writing them. When one sits down to the act of writing it should be accomplished in the spirit of making history. It does require some bit of audacity on the part of the writer to think this result even remotely possible. So much of note has already been written that a writer might even ask herself *why even try*? And the more books a person reads the less confident this realization for completion exists. Instead, it is always *what is next*. What comes after? Next page, next chapter, next book, and always aware of and considering what came before. And ultimately, after all has been said and done, and man manages to finally destroy himself and all of civilization, will this word still remain? Will anything ever written continue to be seen and heard? It may well be known, by then, that *all is vanity*. That everything created was simply a vain attempt. Nothing may survive the catastrophe ahead. The total annihilation of humanity. And nothing left in its stead but a written word and record of its oncoming destruction. It is possible, through Clifford Hagen, that Freddy sees it already coming. The workings behind our unraveling. The loose threads entangled by the curves and crevasses made by our earthly bodies. The alien profundity, released into a dying atmosphere. An interplanetary trajectory loosed upon the universe, on wings, and the awful screeching, born of a multitude of crying and despair.

The image remains with me, having burned itself hard into my brain. Freddy's father Poop-pa brandishing his iron poker, seated in his wheelchair before the fireplace looking to whack someone, anybody, his anger and resentment a menace and scourge to anyone within proximity. Freddy is under the table trembling with fear while Jo-Jo maneuvers his body far enough from the angry old cripple to not get hit. Baby Ruth is standing nearby making wardrobe adjustments to her larger-than-life self. A sculpted and vivid picture of household hostility. No resolution ever, nor any hope for happiness possible. There is no end to this persistent madness. A brother and mother both dead, or at least the preferred alternative to being made prisoner in this home. But none deserve better than they get. And I suppose the final point, the period on this long sentence brought down to bear as justice, falls on the deserving. My wife always reminds me that "You get what you give." And that god-awful truth is ably proven by Clifford Hagen, a fellow who says he "likes girls, fast cars, and bourbon", and who "writes all the time" except for when he isn't. He who has left no evidence of a life after *Sunshine* either for himself, or Freddy.

Chapter 58: The Rhythm of My Black Despair

...All living organisms are condemned to perversity, to the narrowness of being mere fragments of a larger totality that overwhelms them, which they cannot understand or truly cope with — yet must still live and struggle with. ___
Otto Rank from *Art and Artist*

There will be no peace for Freddy amidst all this rain. He will never again know how wonderful and different it feels when the sun begins to warm your body and to dry out your gear. The sun's rays on your bare skin make the deluge and dismal days that came before quickly forgotten. The past, with its awful categories, are swiftly compartmentalized by the comforting sun. Good or bad, nothing ever lasts. But even the good days become a bore without a bit of difficult weather and bouts of bad mood. Better to have a shot of something to kill the pain, or a lick off a sugary spoon. And then we might retreat into our mundane life again with all its generalities and predictable outcomes constantly staring us in the face. Why take risks and perch our toes on the edge of some greater abyss? It is what it always is. At least for the un-resourceful ones among us. John Steinbeck writes a great deal about his good friend Ed Ricketts' non-teleological, or "is" thinking, in his book *The Log from the Sea of Cortez*. Rather than continue questioning everything, Ricketts' emphasis was on why it was more important to accept things as they are. It is natural to always want to know the cause of everything. The motive behind teleological thinking is so you do not make the same mistake again, or find one's self engaged in matters that were the absolutely wrong course. It is extremely difficult to change a lifetime of behavior or a fixed pattern of thinking. As hard as I try I find it almost impossible to change the most entrenched idiosyncrasies that seem to define me. It has been rewarding when I do accept my differences, what genuinely makes me unique in the world, and what *is*. But to actually change something about me that no longer works is often a world-class challenge.

Perhaps there was a particularly momentous day when Clifford Hagen decided for himself to write a novel. He put his scribblings on the page, and each time he sat his body down to write he continued on with where he had left himself off the previous day. Perhaps he had no detailed plan for character development, no outline to speak of, and rarely developed any description of a character that would have anything to do with the stereotypical weight or color of their skin. Southern vernacular would not be exaggerated except in extreme cases in which another countless hint of bigotry or racism would be deemed necessary to further whatever little action the author wanted forwarded. Within this writer's composition there would be no seduction of the reader, and the wanton sexual activity within the household described remained exclusively between those individuals managing the grounds and workings of this home. There was little need for more specific details regarding the constant rain. Its steady pouring resembled coarse salt more than the typical fine watering generally needed for things to abundantly grow. And there would be no metaphors absent the element of despair.

I wonder if Clifford Hagen killed himself, or if Gordon Lish did it for him? If after what had to be a meager and disappointing payday Lish decided the man's life wasn't at all worth it and had the name killed off. There would be no record of his existence unless Harper & Row decided to reveal the mystery behind the history of this novel and the man who wrote it. Through the years Gordon repeatedly expressed to me how profitable his ghostwriting activities were for him, and to his critics I point out the many different styles of writing Lish imposed on the books authored by him but which lack, by design, his name on the cover.

Chapter 59: The Non-Returning Tide

There are many respectable, well-meaning and productive members of our society who appreciate the arts and sciences who, for whatever reason, finally end their life by suicide. Perhaps Freddy's mama wanted to end her life too but for the longest time had not the fortitude to do herself in and chose instead to lose herself somewhere within the confines of her mind. It seems that hopelessness can be an affliction too overwhelming for some of us and we become desperate for it to stop. Others choose a slower way to die through the abusive use of alcohol or drugs, and maybe even cigarettes as another absurd destructive vehicle of choice. Maybe even over-eating is a more socially acceptable way of committing suicide. But the ones who take the extreme route through a bloody or violent death always get the most attention. Why the majority of Freddy's family chose to continue existing in an obviously hopeless situation is maddening to me. At least in most portrayals of patients in mental homes there are some with smiles on their faces or at least observed as being engaged in a playful activity. There was no fun happening in Freddy's house. Only a bit of lecherous behavior by the adults, and sand crab hunting and mutilations being performed by Freddy. As hopeless as this family seemed to be I am surprised there was no murder being committed. But perhaps there was and it had to do with the unreported fate of Freddy's younger, dead brother.

I am finally, it seems, coming to the end of my quest. It is the lesser of my understanding rather than my hoped-for resolution. It may come as no surprise that Freddy's household is not aware of their dire situation and the utter futility of a life no longer worth living. Surely there is someone in their vicinity who can finish them off for good. It is doubtful the crippled old fool Poop-pa can reach them with his iron poker or even get a decent swing to take off their heads. And for me to consider leaving Freddy forever in hiding, trembling under the family's kitchen table is unacceptable. And though I am hesitant to use the word *aghast* it may be close to what I am feeling for Hagen's failure, or resistance, to put these people out of their misery. Perhaps it is better for me to remain in false belief that Gordon Lish wrote this buggering masterpiece of confusion and despair. It is doubtful however that Gordon would have let these matters rest without a proper burial. Where is the truth to be found in any of Hagen's text that reveals again that we are always in the state of becoming? Perhaps it is too late for him, old age besting the worst of his ideas. Gordon Lish will continue to create what it is he wants to be remembered for, and meanwhile I pretend to wait.

Having gone to my own well, I am adrift and without consolation. I continue to see a posturing Lish standing in for Clifford Hagen. I am cast out though, relying only on my memory. Must we hold on and exclaim to others, who sometimes matter, that these remembrances did at one time exist as experience, and who is it who can question the validity of these matters? A resemblance between his life and fiction should not be at all surprising. Any thorough examination of all the different texts authored by Gordon Lish would provide ample proof for what is claimed by many who came in contact with him. A student first, wanting to be a published author, would go to almost any length in providing what was required for a writer to get into print. And that might include not only the strongest of words produced on the page but also an infidelity, and a dismissal for monogamy especially. The most remarkable claims for whom the great Lish has sexually bedded relies most heavily on the curious fact that these women he took to his bed, for the most part, were already taken by another. And he gained more satisfaction the following morning knowing these women returning to their homes were married to somebody else. There was a great pride in his unseemly victories over, and against, these other men, and it made his tales of sexual encounters more respectable in light of the jeopardy his lurid acts imposed. A requirement, I might add, present in all his fiction.

Chapter 60: The Aroma of Freshly Mowed Grass

Gordon Lish often makes disparaging comments about writers that he believes he may have helped in the past, who have now gone their separate way, who might have garnered some fame or recognition for their work but then fail to credit Lish with his helping them, or bestow him ample enough credit due to their success. In my experience with Gordon there is little that bothers him more than this perceived affront. And because of this his name will never be absent from the opening pages of anything I ever write or have published. I will always and forever give him full credit for what I have become as both a writer and a person, acknowledging what he has done for me, and what a great friend to me he always was. Writing poetry was the one thing I was surprisingly gifted at producing, and for the time I spent intimately involved with composing it I produced no few remarkable specimens still unrecognized by those who decide the value or greatness of certain literary endeavors. But I know the poems will one day measure up to historical standards, and that is good enough for me. But I have always desired to be an author of much longer works of prose and to write about what matters most to me. My poems, generally, were simply brilliant and delightful uses of language. More fun and games than serious. A *good time* is how Gordon generally phrased it. And Gordon never encouraged me to write prose. Even within his greatest accomplishments as editor he has much too often disparaged the work of authors he previously championed. Even Raymond Carver has been disparaged by Lish who, in recently published interviews, has said that he did not consider Carver to be *much of anything in the long run.* I am of contrary opinion by holding that the human condition has never been more honestly examined by any other writer when compared to the works of Raymond Carver. Carver is King, and thank God, Gordon Lish made him so.

Dear darling Michael,

I can't--lend myself to touching the infamous evidence of your kindness to me--not with a ten-foot pole could I touch it, man. But I can say, with all my heart, hooray for your fighting the fight. All this fever of yours, the sand, the fire, the strictness to have it as you sense it must be had, don't you know it impels you in the making of your poetries, your gorgeous poetries?

G

Roth is full of shit," he says without hesitation. Jonathan Franzen is undeserving of his reputation, as is Jonathan Lethem. The postmodernist Lydia Davis is "ridiculously overrated." Paul Auster, too: "I can't read him anymore." The subtle redesign of The New Yorker has been a "dreadful error." The upstart Brooklyn lit mag n+1 is a "crock of shit".___Gordon Lish, Newsweek: An Angry Flash of Gordon by Alexander Nazaryan / June 19, 2014

Chapter 61: Sex as an Episode

Another short fiction in the wide-ranging oeuvre
of Gordon Lish is titled *My True Story* and it
provides a list of all the women he, the Gordon
Lish of the story, has had sex with throughout his
life up until his marriage to his last wife, Barbara.
It is a long list. Gordon has a reputation among
his still-growing stable of writers and students as
quite a prolific lover of women. Some argue that
it is a rather unhealthy posture to take, and
theorized by some as founded on a homophobic
makeup of extremes in wanting to prove himself a
manly man. The fact is, Gordon today is a frail
and rather thin man who has written often enough
of walking on the high side of sloped city
sidewalks in order to make himself appear taller
than he is. He also credits all powerful writers as
having superior bodies than their smaller
contemporaries, thus affording them the physical
endurance needed to continue to write strongly
well after the typical writer has already spent
himself. Having had a long history as being a
proponent of female writers the likes of Amy

Hemphill and others he has taught, my experience has it that Lish's emphasis has mostly veered more to the male writer. Even in regards to myself and my beginnings, focussed on wanting to write short stories, Lish, when faced with my first poem, insisted I stick with prose and cautioned that *poetry is for sissies*. Eventually he changed his position. He began instead to champion my poetry and subsequently counseled that I stick with poems as he believed I was a "natural born poet". But the public statements in all of Lish's teachings are on his emphasis to *stay hard*, be strong, and to fuck as often as you can. I considered his relating to me, and others, of his latest sexual escapades as seeds meant to germinate possible stories for him. That is, until he announced to me that he had finally quit writing and that love-making, and specifically the art of fucking, was his new career and chosen art form. He began referring to his concubines as "clients" and even before that they were regularly labeled as his "pipe cleaners". And in my eyes there was nothing wrong with that. I enjoyed hearing about it. And as my wife's and my relationship evolved and strengthened with Gordon Lish, we as well considered her joining into his sexual fray. The fact that Gordon lived in what can only be described as an art gallery or museum of fine effects, and the details of great attention Gordon related to us as he insured a memorable, though night-long experience of lovemaking with these women, it was not hard to imagine my wife enjoying herself immensely and at the same time standing in for me, as my surrogate, thanking Lish for being such a good and reliable friend.

Chapter 62: The Place Marked Exit

Standing in the hallway of Gordon Lish's apartment, across from his library a few steps off the kitchen, I noticed on the nearest shelf to me a book that I had lent him a few months prior to my New York visit titled *Essays Critical and Clinical* written by Gilles Deleuze. It was Deleuze's final work before he committed suicide due to his debilitating health. I initially purchased the hardcover first printing at the cost of fifty dollars. But Gordon said that as he was reading my copy he had written so many notes in the margins that he could no longer return the book to me, or pry himself away from this artifact. As much as I wanted him to give it back to me I reasoned that this was the least I could offer him for all his trouble in helping me, for his friendship bestowed upon me through the past several years, and he, here now, allowing my wife and I into his private lair. His apartment resembled a museum of fine antique furniture and accessories, clean as a whistle, and he quite proud of this abode and willing to give us a casual tour of his surroundings. In his bedroom, at the foot of his bed before the large-screen TV, I stood there reminded of what I knew he put on this screen, imagining the fantastic sexual performance of Rocco Siffredi and Aga, about the many years I had considered offering my wife to him as well for his sexual pleasure, our collaboration together in establishing a plan for this eventual encounter, and here we were spontaneously inside his home for the very first time, surprised, and with no idea how to proceed.

For years my wife and I practiced our seduction of Gordon Lish as required of him. My writing, my poetry, almost on a weekly basis sent to him in sleeves of three. Pages meant to seduce the teacher into wanting to read more from me and to champion my endeavors. In the meantime my wife would allow, from time to time, a nude photograph of herself to also be mailed to him, perhaps with a personal note attached, and we would then expect his personal message returned to her on a postcard leading into, what he certainly made no point in denying, a promising and eventful sexual foray. It was fun, and productive, while it lasted. It was not obscene at all but instead a serious attempt at creating art, and the final scene one in which we might all triumphantly enjoy. Given the man's age at this writing, reason would insist he is now too old and frail for this type of rough and tumble engagement he had so often described to me in our many conversations. But the fantasy of sharing my wife sexually with Gordon Lish did exist enough to sustain our interest in continuing on with our theatrics as collaborators, and eventually allow us the freedom and confidence to move on without him, minus the filtering of Lish, and less the mediation constricting my own obsessions impelling me take action in creating art apart from him. In other words, Gordon prepared me for my exodus.

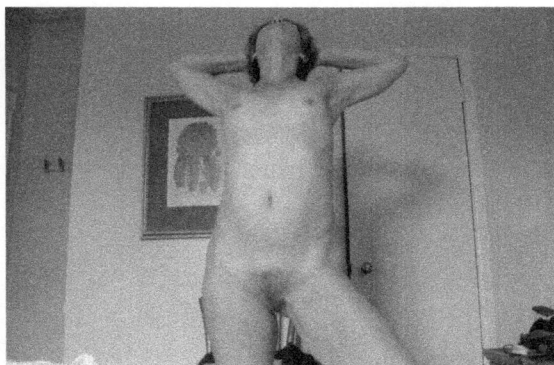

Chapter 63: The Umbrella is My Friend

*Rain is coming, that's how it feels.*___Sam Baker, *The Tattooed Woman*

There is no sudden catastrophe or imminent danger the reader has been exposed to in *Sunshine*. Just the constant drumming of the rain and the potential hurricane predicted for the vicinity. Basically the same hopeless situation permeates the entire household for the duration of this short novel. Nothing about their pitiable condition abates or ever appears palatable. It is possible that Clifford Hagen enlisted The Grim Reaper to stand behind them all, same as the Reaper also quietly stalks our daily lives no matter how successful we think we are at keeping this ghoul at bay. We seem to always be waiting for the other shoe to drop. Or our denial is so thick we avoid even thinking these awful thoughts. Perhaps we are so busy we do not hear or feel His presence behind everything we do. It is said we will know *not the time nor the place*. Maybe we are so engaged in what we call "the good life" that we are unaware of its coming end. But then it happens, or threatens to, and all bets are off except for those of us still left with gratitude for our chance at living. But for this result, Freddy was not made. Instead, every shape or form of pain engulfs him until he becomes as mean as his father. He rails against the black hired help, and screams and taunts them with racial slurs he has heard his father use. Just another nut falling not far from the tree. A legacy continued. Another monster in the making. An irresponsible ridicule for anything that matters and lays its claim on goodness and light. A drenching rain that never ends. A violence created by Hagen's steady measures on the page. A *forever* worth noting and preparing to escape from.

Perhaps the message to be found in *Sunshine* is that it makes little sense for us to go on. That life is hopeless and not worth the time. Several years back I had my own struggle with the meaning of life. And at dinner at a Mexican restaurant Lish frequents near his home on 96th Street, he gestured with his hands, as if to envelop my entire family gathered there around the table and said, *"This is meaning. Being together, sharing a meal and conversation."* And I knew that he was right.

The winning of any good race involves either being the swiftest of all, or lucky. It was good fortune that I have had Gordon Lish as both my editor and friend for over twenty years. I have been criticized for continuing after all these years to allow Gordon to have the final say on whether an individual poem of mine was worthy, or not, to be published. But our collaborative discipline was a good one as it pushed me to produce the best possible work I could. His teaching always impressed upon the endless well deep within all of us, that mediocrity in any form was unacceptable, and that by tossing those less than suitable creations into the trash would free us to get to the next one unencumbered by some faulty need to save everything as if they all mattered. He showed me the truth of his teachings in his own practice. Gordon Lish is so severe in his posture, in this insistent stance he models everyday. My decision to veer away from poetry, or advance my writing in another direction than what he approved of, did not sit well with him. Our almost weekly (and at times daily) telephone conversations trickled to a stop. No longer would we meet-up at a local sandwich shop when I made my annual trip into the city. Nor would he call to ask my hand in finding him a book title he had heard of, or a rare porn flick he was intent on viewing. I would not be privy anymore to tales of his latest sexual conquest. But I know the relationship we did have for all those years was something nobody can ever take away from me, and one that few others would have the pleasure of enjoying as I did. Gordon Lish is certainly a man of several identities, a personality similar to the one the artist Ray Johnson portrayed in the Lish film favorite *How to Draw a Bunny*. It would be difficult for me to believe Gordon wanted his sexual conquests to remain a secret between us. Anyone who has attended a Lish fiction-writing class has to know he maintained few filters on what he told stories about. Especially about people he knew. No personal secret was ever safe with Gordon Lish.

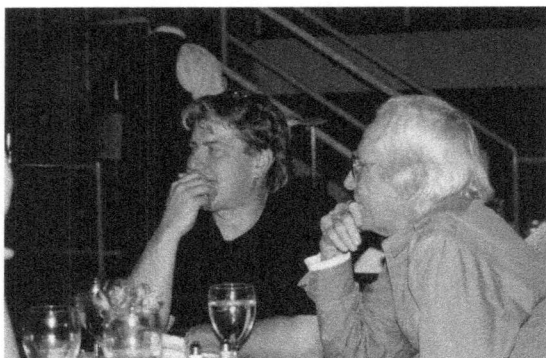

Chapter 64: The Very End of a Long Black Ribbon

*... I feel in the anemone lady a strange attraction to sex. There is in me a masculine element that, when I am thinking of her, arises and overshadows all the others... "Why am I not a man," I say to the sand and barrenness with a certain strained, tense passion, "that I might give this wonderful, dear, delicious woman an absolutely perfect love!"*___Mary MacLane, *March 5* from *I Await the Devil's Coming*

Discovering the writings of Mary MacLane has freed me to examine more precisely my own love for Gordon Lish, or what I perceived this love to be. I confess, somewhat shamefully, though I know not why, to my being for several years *in love* with Gordon Lish. Not in a sexual way, but so full of gratitude for what he did for me, my family, and the evolving relationship with my wife because of all our newfound interests due to Lish's history, encouragement, and instruction. I felt so much gratitude for his helping me to see what art truly is, to finally know in my heart I could produce it, and to have the courage to be myself on the page. The risks I took in composing each poem, the way in which I progressed onto my literary destiny, all because of Gordon Lish. The world became much larger for me, a universe full of great men and women I finally had access to. No longer was I a lost young man stuck in a small extinct lumber town on the banks of Lake Huron. And because of this immense love and gratitude I felt for Gordon Lish there was something inside me needing physical expression. And my examination of a potential personal manifestation proved uneventful due to my inherent cowardly essence. I went on to imagine myself a woman with a vagina which did me no good. I had no desire at all for Gordon to sexually penetrate me. And so I imagined the opposite and again felt nothing resembling attraction to my penetrating him. The only alternative that felt correct was our both sharing, if she was willing, the attentions of my great wife. It was the only gift I might give that was worthy of my love for him. There was no other person nor expression fit for his total consumption. The only thing I could think of to further enhance our relationship was for Gordon to have his own sexual engagement with her, to bed my wife as surrogate to me. And by her own hand, nude photographs mailed to him offered a promising seduction. Their playful dance proceeded for years with the idea of eventual accomplishment. It was only fitting. There could be no other way into the totality of this man. And for her I believed it would be an opportunity of a lifetime, to momentarily live life on the edge, to step out of her rather mundane life with me and the typical requirements of a monogamous marriage, and to do so with my blessing.

...*Anticipation is the mother of invention. And in his (Rousseau's) commitment to innocence there is always the covert suggestion that nothing is forbidden, that we are not controlling ourselves, just finding ways of making what we don't do more exciting...In order to fall in love with someone they must be perceived to be an obstacle, a necessary obstacle...it is the obstacle that makes possible the object, that makes possible the idea of someone else...I know what something or someone is by finding out what comes between us...Obstacles are the clue to*

desire...the world is full of meaning. ___Adam
Phillips from *Looking at Obstacles*

Many novels and short stories have been written
about adulterous activities, and for one specific
occasion we wanted to make it an *is* for ourselves.
The idea gradually tempted both of us until it
became an almost guaranteed eventuality and we
seriously considered the consequences.
Something was wrong. What of all the many
women Gordon had already claimed to have bed?
In our research regarding promiscuous activity we
learned of the increased chance of contracting a
sexually transmitted disease, that Beverly would
in essence be having sex with every woman
Gordon ever had sex with. And if she did
contract an STD our marriage would be ruined
rather than enhanced, and we had serious doubts
about what would be left of our union if the affair
went south. The threat of disease did become the
ultimate deal-breaker, though there were other
concerns involved in the decision as well, due to
my own feelings of inferiority and the shame that
could possibly permeate our lives. More even
than the threat of contracting a sexual disease,
there was an attitude, perhaps a posture of
entitlement that evolved within a spirit of
unequals. It became a power move, a mentor's
conquest that I feared would unfairly be bragged
about, and the truth forever forgotten because of
his great name. It was my name, and her name,
that would decide our fate. We no longer deemed
it important or prudent to consummate this other
marriage. Instead, by my own hand, I forced an
amicable divorce. Falling off my cabin roof

became its impetus.

Chapter 65: The Grotesque Parody of Our Lives

Annie Ernaux began her novel *Shame* with the words, *My father tried to kill my mother one Sunday in June ...* and then never mentions it again, and instead adroitly details a child's life in which we might understand why she introduced her work with those words. Ernaux certainly identifies with her shame, and has done so since the age of twelve. She says she carries it with her even to this day. As foreign as this concept may at first seem, and as important as the personal questions are that follow, her identity, I deduced from reading this book, is based on the connection made between the shame she has carried since the age of twelve and the intensely heightened emotional and physical sensation she experiences to this day through orgasm. Discovering this concept of hers near the end of *Shame* certainly made it novel. But, as yet, I have not completely gotten my head around the connection she makes between shame and orgasm, at least on a feeling level for myself.

Chapter 66: Pregnant Again with the Unwanted

*...The geniuses are always more human than the herd.*___Mary MacLane from *I Await the Devil's Coming*

During the last six weeks I have not only discovered the writer Mary MacLane but also Jessa Crispin. And finding MacLane was solely due to the work of my reading Crispin. And other surprising writers are sure to follow, and mostly women it seems. After five decades of reading mainly the work of males I am forcefully drawn to words of women. It is as if I have no choice but to devour these brilliant compositions. And though the mantle of *feminism* is attached to these ladies I find them energetically honest and forthright with no malice intended on the face of their words. It often cannot be helped that deceivers with agendas attach labels and interpret works to fit their needs. What is refreshing about the century-old person of MacLane and the contemporary voice of Crispin is their position in their own worlds as equal haters. No woman nor man is safe from the barbs of either. They penetrate our bullshit and reveal the truths behind our masks. They both create exhilarating and exciting books for us to read and offer insights into other writers we may have missed ourselves due to previous indoctrinations, education, and our individual upbringing.

Perhaps Mary MacLane was too brazen in her stated positions. She did not wilt, nor did she acquiesce to anyone. She was a creature on her own in a world separate from the one she knew so intimately. As fraudulent as she felt herself to be in regards to what was expected of her, she nonetheless remained as true to herself as she possibly could. She died young at forty-eight and I want to know why.

Chapter 67: In the Fires of a Hundred Sleepless Nights

The perhaps shameful but all-too-real fantasy of my wife having an extramarital affair with Gordon Lish carried on harmlessly for years before good reasoning helped us decide against ultimately going through with it. But the idea itself always remained present and expressive within the act of our lovemaking. Talking through every risk while having sex made for more lively encounters and excitement in our bed. But it is also true that the resulting orgasm abruptly ended the fantasy as it immediately interrupts that marvelous train of thought. That is why orgasm is called "the little death". I cannot express enough the number of times I used my fantasy of Gordon Lish fucking my wife even as her naked body was spread over me, her legs astride my hips, her pelvis rhythmically rocking and gyrating, raising the level of her involvement to involuntary aggressiveness. But this *little death* always temporarily killed me, emptying me of every illicit and delicious thought I ever had. In fact, after having sex, I was often horrified at the thought of sharing my wife with anyone. It frightened and was threatening to me that perhaps she would enjoy these trysts so much that I would lose her to these newly awakened sexual impulses and I would ultimately have no one but myself to blame. But upon initiating any new sex in the upcoming days this vivid and celebratory fantasy would return to make our love-making enriched and most satisfying again until that fateful *death of me* would occur again and the process revealed for another time as a flawed and dangerous idea to everyone concerned, especially myself. The greatest threat was in potentially losing her I suppose, but if I were to be as honest as can be, there was really nothing to fear if she maintained her love for me. And believe me when I say I truly wish I *could* share her, and at the same time remain feeling whole and unthreatened. But that person is obviously not me, nor the woman called my wife who could perform that behavior sober and not have the accompanying shame and regret she was so positive would follow.

Chapter 68: She Had No Truck with Sweets

A few years ago Gordon suggested to my wife and I that we watch Rocco Siffredi's porno film *Rocco Invades Poland*. There is a segment somewhere in the middle of the action in which Rocco and his cohorts are fucking any willing participant available for the camera. There is nothing too exciting at the beginning of this scene. But suddenly a young Polish girl enters the room, blond with porcelain skin, not one of the original girls initially interviewed at the beginning of the film, and Rocco quickly notices her as she is undressed and begins to get pummeled by one of his buddies. And because Rocco is the star of the series he decides to take her for his own. What entails is the longest, most vigorous event of sexual endurance and performance ever put on screen. At least that I have ever seen. On first viewing, a mounting fear is present for this young girl named Aga for her ultimately becoming a sacrificial victim due to Rocco's violent fucking. This murderous, on-the-edge tension proves to sustain itself throughout the entire episode. But little Aga holds her own against this monster of a man as he rams his giant appendage inside of her in every position imaginable. Fact is, Aga seems to suggest she wants even more, that she can take whatever he has to give her, and no matter how hard Rocco fucks her she does not wilt nor does she succumb to any of his aggressivity. She seems even to willingly egg him on with an agreeableness for sustaining anything he possibly has in store for her. At one point near the end of the act, a sweating and exhausted Rocco turns to face the camera and says to some effect, *This is not kidding. What you are watching is real!* Even the glass table top remains unbroken even though the weight and force of their wild fucking should have shattered it to smithereens. My wife and I both maintain, with Gordon, that this is the best porno scene ever made. And we saw the film as a message from Gordon as to what my wife might expect if she actually went through with our fantasy. And precisely as parallel to Clifford Hagen, Aga, after one significant performance, would never be seen, nor found again, regardless of the intensity and extent of our online search.

M. Sarti
621 Cochran Hill Rd.
Louisville, Ky
40206

please call to read
me "Afterward" if
in final form, or
mail it _ 2) The
blonde in "K. I. Island"
is named "Agnes". Let's
see if she shows up
in something else, okay?
All thanks for all
help.

Chapter 69: She Danced with a Feather Fan

Near the beginning of the book *Mirages, The Unexpurgated Diary of Anaïs Nin 1939-1947,* Nin made an entry regarding her move to New York City to escape the German war threatening Paris. She relates an incident that she was involved in while riding in a crowded subway car. Standing, as we are all wont to do in these congested instances, and holding one of the floor-to-ceiling metal bars for balance and support, she noticed a tall man with his back to her. The rail car was packed so everyone was pressed up against each other. Anaïs Nin felt the hand of this man brush against her sex. As was her custom, she was not wearing any undergarments And she was not sure if the man had intended to touch her there, but she decided to take a chance and so pressed her sex back into his free and dangling hand. He responded by discreetly caressing her now-wet genitals, working his fingers underneath her dress and eventually inside her vagina. Nin never saw the man's face, as his back remained always in front of her. And when the subway made its next scheduled stop he exited the train and she never saw him again. This was not an everyday common occurrence as Anaïs Nin routinely rode these trains and never again entered into her diary another subway incident even remotely resembling this one.

Chapter 70: A Vulgar Immortality

...It took me a lifetime to be able to enjoy a man without love... Anaïs Nin, *Mirages, The Unexpurgated Diary of Anaïs Nin 1939-1947*

My wife would send Gordon naked pictures of herself as gifts to enjoy, which he did, and he was always appreciative of them. From time to time she would include a personal note and he did the same in return. If my wife was not attractive, or unwilling to share naked photos of herself with Gordon, I doubt any of my fantasies would have had a chance at becoming a possibility. But because she did send him these loving notes and naked pictures of herself he became more than interested. The idea of them being together developed into more than simply a possibility, and now it was only a matter of when. Gordon lived in New York and we lived in Louisville. It became harder for him to travel and eventually he gave up on the idea of ever making it out of the city again. My wife and I did visit New York religiously every autumn. I always let him know of our plans and that I, or we, certainly wanted to get together for a bite to eat and conversation. But eventually our visits became something else. It felt as if a promise had been made and gone back on. The seductive affair began to frame and expose a person being used for advantage, whether it be art or conquest in an unspoken battle. What once we heartily accepted as being willing participants in making another notch on Gordon's bedpost became for us instead a disgusting proposition. This eventual soiling of my wife became something permanent and unsavory to me. It was a chance I could not take. And my wife agreed with me. But we could not end our obsessive fantasy and the enjoyment we got out of our continued imagining. So even though we decided not to go through with it, the possibility always remained.

Listen, pal, I'm sorry
but I'm just a sucker
for what you do. Your
play works me into a
trance. Hooray for all
its conditions. One could
quibble with this and
that, but then one beholds
some teensiness (a dwell-
ing, an _indwelling_) and
forgives, forgets, submits to
all. Tell B, she dances,
fidgets, insinuates her course
into slumber just as I
(seek to] do. It is only
when I am engaged in an
embrace that I can →

The greatest development in this whole affair is

that the three of us remained friends. There was surprisingly never any bitter or hurtful feelings. And for some time after our failure I continued to send him additional nude photographs of *the one who got away*. The new poems I mailed to him still featured certain fantasies I would always keep foremost in mind. Beverly expressed in her inscription to him how she so appreciated his eyes on her, but acknowledged as well the failure of her first test that night at the restaurant, and she offered up her personal hope of graduating with an eventual degree. He answered us with his typical prompt and lovely postcard, thanking us for the gift and expressing, *Every reason to hope you will be graduated Summa Cum Laude.*

But afterwards sickness and poor timing with Gordon became the new norm whenever we arrived for our annual pilgrimages to his great city. A recent virus, or a surgery to cut away his threatening skin cancer, left him recovering from what it was that ailed him, and he would announce he was no longer available to meet up with us for a lunch or dinner together. I wearied of fighting the drug-induced stupor Gordon demonstrated too often on the phone. No longer was his great voice full of energy and expounding on his latest female conquest. Sadly he became to me a tired old man, drugged to sleep, and always battling some sickness or another. Our relationship had finally begun to become a fading memory. And perhaps something to be denied and in time claimed to have never happened. But had he been afforded his sexual event with my wife I believe there would have been no end to the conversation. He would have told everyone in his circle. Gordon does not keep secrets except if they have to do with himself, or might cause him to be put in grave danger. In these most threatening cases he expects you as well to keep his secrets too. But this triangular affair of ours is something I have tried for years to come to some closure with. The whys and why nots have disturbed me for too long. There are reasons for relationships to come to some commingling, whether consummated or not.

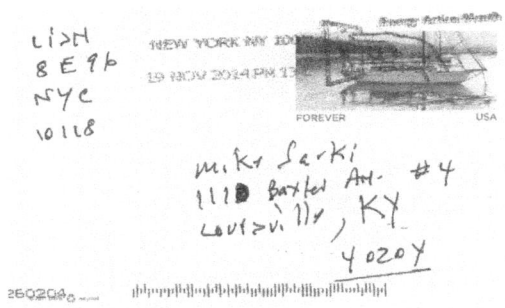

Trouble. Eyes, They
are shot. Can't do
much reading/writing.
But just finished Cess,
out from O/K early spring,
of no account alongside
it's novel. Way! But
that we have sons who
are surpassing us.

Sorry to hear of your
difficulties. Yet you
must not meet them
with depression.
making things — that's my
anything consolation — that
only noodle. All best
and to you.

Chapter 71: Fine Words Butter No Parsnips

In 1937, at the age of sixteen, Bianca Bienenfeld
became a student of Simone de Beauvoir. A
triad evolved, which included Simone de
Beauvoir's concomitant Jean-Paul Sartre, in
which they eventually deflowered her. When war
broke out and the trio was forced to dissolve,
permanent emotional damage was inflicted on
Bienenfeld. Having sex with Bienenfeld while

engaged in a quasi-parental relationship with her broke a long-standing incestual taboo. This untoward behavior eventually traumatized young Bienenfeld and resulted in severe anxiety and constant weeping. Simone de Beauvoir always felt responsible and guilty for what had happened. In my own particularities there are as well moments when I consider what I may have purposely inflicted on my wife had we accomplished the goals of my fantasies. But though I suggested these salacious fantasies, I was always careful to make clear to her what was perhaps at stake if we were to actually go through with one of these sexual adventures. Of course there would be no end to the blame and shame if the event turned disastrous. And though we all eventually became friends as well as associates, I have to think there was something of a similar Bienenfeld parental relationship with us being involved with Gordon Lish on such a personal level. And he being twenty years our senior did add the incestual quotient to our affair and is something that must, at the least, be considered.

There were always emotional ties involved in the many sexual relations both Simone de Beauvoir and Anaïs Nin describe. What matters most however were the compartments these certain sexual unions occupied. It was necessary to both women that love and sex remain emotionally appropriate. Sensuality was not to be confused with love, even though the connection may be made within the sex act. But having sex with fire was not necessarily related at all to being emotionally involved with someone they were not in love with. Many times, in fact, they were the exact opposite. And this is what I wished for us. It was my hope that Beverly, in our proposed and sanctioned infidelity, would be sensually set on fire but remain herself in love with me, and grateful for a sexual experience so unnatural to her thinking, so salacious and satisfying that her body would, at times, demand her newly-awakened sexual hunger be assuaged again. Already present in her I have witnessed components of this sexual animal I fantasized myself creating. I was never attempting to make of her something she was not, in fact it is myself whom I have prepped for change. And to this eventual effect there will never be a final accident, nor any resolution I can ever depend on. It is the same reason many lives of long accomplishment relate themselves to successions of every stripe, their somewhat pointless mappings of their plans, and matters reluctantly arranged through intensely-focussed avoidances for a chaotic trajectory one can never be certain of surviving. This extended, but still ultimate failure, having been by this time so verbosely objectified among these many pages, I claim now as our own. And I have refused to allow this failure to remain hidden, instead projecting it as our own hand-made noose, swinging rhythmically in the wind as if religiously hung from our perpetual tree of shame we find impossible to escape from.

Chapter 72: One Pale Curl of Foam

Sunshine comes and it goes. I wrote what I thought would be my last letter to Gordon, and he responded to it favorably.

20 March 2015

Dear Gordon,

Life is good here in Florida for me. I have spent enough time down here to know firsthand this is a strange and exotic land. Often I am alone, working on this house we purchased as a project to ward off my winter demons, dark tormentors that woefully harass me in Kentucky. Beverly teaches children part-time in Louisville to help supplement these creative endeavors. I feel fortunate to have her, at least in spirit, if not always in the flesh. After almost four years of frustrating struggle I believe she has finally moved beyond her troubled hand.

I want to apologize to you for the honest desires and fantasies of mine that never came to anything. For all these many years, since being introduced to you, I have used these same fantasies and obsessions in my writing in order to seduce you, the teacher, as I knew was required of me as your student. I did not know that my continued practice of seduction would one day lead me to an even further event which I demanded of myself, and my wife, that this virtual seduction be demonstrated physically. I am to this day still disappointed that neither Beverly nor myself were actually able to go through with our planned affair. There are times I feel ashamed of myself for involving you in what could be wrongly perceived as a deception. I am not sure today if it was my own manhood I found lacking, or my need to pretend I was somebody other than the coward I truly am. But I do believe Beverly and I did honestly apply ourselves seriously to partaking in this infidelity, and the reality of our pathetic retardation I unabashedly blame on a grippingly subjugated Christian upbringing. But I still dream of possibilities, as they unhaltingly nurture the enjoyment of my days.

Gordon, I have nothing but fond memories for our old relationship. The many phone calls made and received, the reports of your almost countless sexual conquests, your writing, health, and clever anecdotes which involved such a wide range of affairs. Throughout the last eleven months I have been engaged in writing extensively about this

*relationship with you, my personal failures, how I
came to know you, and what you have meant to
me as a writer, a friend, my teacher, and editor. I
have examined also within my writing the
previous years I spent attempting to seduce you
on the page as required. In my poetry I attempted
to courageously get to the abyss you so often
spoke of in class, and if I failed at my efforts and
did not succeed, I wished at least to come to the
brink of that precipice in which my balance, or
lack of, might allow me to hover a bit on the edge
or tumble freestyle into the darkest of these very
pits. And that was my first version of jeopardy,
and history must, and will, agree I did succeed.
But the same good luck and fortune has been
absent with my prose fiction, and thus, this life of
mine, sometimes lived, has become what I choose
instead now to save historically, if there is to be
any. I have always publicly championed you as
the truest artist and friend I have ever known.
And it is my wish that by the time I have
completed this project that I will also have done
justice to your greatness in every facet you chose
to make me privy to during our time together.*

*I feel so privileged to have known you, to have
shared meals, concerns, and even pictures of my
naked wife with you. With your consent,
encouragement, and loving appreciation you
afforded Beverly several hours of personal
pleasure and satisfaction. You made her feel
more sexy and appreciated as a woman than I
alone was capable of. I know for her that sharing
her nude photographs and films with you was
very gratifying, and something she would never*

*have done with any other. Obviously our
seductions directed at you were potentially
dangerous to the monogamy of our marriage. But
the resulting infidelity, as ironic as it seems, was
warmly considered basically safe because of your
unfailing appreciation for our amateur, though
gamely, attempts at tantalizing you. I do not think
any of this behavior is something to be ashamed
of, but what is important is how Beverly and I
failed to take this playful activity to its rightful,
and predictable, conclusion. It now affords me
countless days of thinking, study and application,
in my unceasing effort to conceptualize the truth
behind our failure. The fact that nothing ever
happened only adds to my obsessive
consternation. Of course, all this could simply be
another fiction, as memory is certainly suspect.
But if there ever was a man I truly wanted to
share my wife with, it was you. And it saddens me
sometimes that it never happened.*

*My wish for you is that you can go on for many
years living a healthy life saturated with literary
and sexual adventure. That is what I, in turn,
desire for myself. But neither one of us is the man
we once were. We do the best we can.*

*Lovingly,
M*

Mike Jarki
PO Box 1851
Melbourne, FL

...2 - 1851

Yes, Mike, it
seems the lesson
to be learned by
all — everybody,
even the seeming
slouches all around
us, is trying his
best. Thank you
for your
letters. You know I
wish you and B,
every good fortune.

Chapter 73: Unfashioned Wedlock

Closure often takes time to emerge as understanding. What I routinely perceived as another failure in my efforts to finally come to some reckoning regarding *Sunshine*, Gordon Lish, and my unwavering desire for a truly wanton adultery slowly developed, what is often the case, into the unexpected. Another fruitless endeavor provided me with a clearer picture of my history with my wife and allowed me a wonderful opportunity to get to know her better. My writing in many ways became a celebration and testament of our great love for each other. It enabled me to glorify her with photography and text as well as offering a public stage in which our secret became our act.

But personal injuries and poor health prevented me from completing this project. My own recovery from the fall off the roof of my cabin in 2010 afforded so many opportunities to question our every salacious motive, and then my wife tumbled as well the following year as she attempted to save our untethered young puppy from getting run over on a busy road. And so, for the last five years we have been trying to find neurological answers for what happened to her, and the medical professionals have failed us miserably. It has been a living hell of nerve pain, involuntary muscle movements, and the sensation of her feeling perpetually tied down. Her soft tissue is similar to a sticky glue that hardened as rock, and rash-like eruptions of the first degree. Sex lives and erotic fantasies take a back seat

when faced with losing one's health. And even
when some progress is believed to have been
made, a new challenge seems to always surface
which immediately questions the validity of our,
perhaps, false hope. But go on we must, slowly
one foot in front of the other.

Gordon Lish is also in bad shape at this writing.
His health is failing. His return correspondence
has come down to brief messages written on
return envelopes,

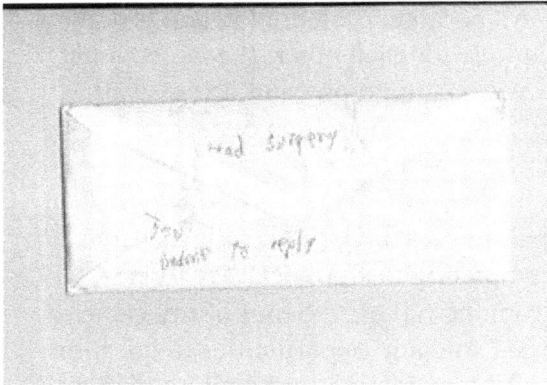

...or even one short sentence on a sticky note
given as reply.

Since
surgery,

not
active.

It is sad to think our time together has truly
ended, but I am afraid our relationship is nearing
its close and will soon be extinguished. Lessons
in life seem to always return us to the realization
there really are few answers to our examinations
and result in further questions. And though it was
silly for me to think it might be otherwise, my
appended failure was certainly worth the time.

*...To throw away the doll was to impose an
obstacle, and by doing so to find out something
about the object.*___Adam Phillips from *Looking
at Obstacles*

Afterword

*...it is sexual desire that is the something about ourselves that makes us untrustworthy, uncivil. It is this that has made our sexuality mad, bad, and dangerous to know...their selfishness, the ruthlessness of their satisfaction...*___from *Going Sane: Maps of Happiness* by Adam Phillips

*Being whole, being sealed and purified and perfect, soaked in bleach and boiled to sterility, is the opposite of life. To breathe is to sully oneself. It's kind of the point.*___from *Reading the Tarot* by Jessa Crispin

*The self does not know anything except its own feelings, and while projecting these feelings it creates its own world.*__ Nikolai Kulbin

Anna wants a party. She makes the proposition to me quite frankly as we are sitting in a cafe one afternoon. She would like to arrange to have a few very dear friends fuck her by wholesale some evening soon ... very soon. From now on it's to be take what you want and to Hell with being something you don't want to be. This is not the Anna as I knew her a few months ago, but Anna has changed a great deal in a short time. One thing, she makes a perfect type for the sort of thing she proposes ... she looks and acts like a lady, she's neat as a pin, dresses well and has some money. In other words, she enjoys all the expensive necessities for conducting herself like a ten-franc whore. ___Henry Miller, *Opus Pistorum*

*...We need, in other words, to know something about what we don't get, and about the importance of not getting it...It is Freud's view that we are excessively disturbed by what we will miss out on if we try to enact an unacceptable desire.*___Adam Phillips from *Missing Out*

It is my belief that most people contain and control their secret obsessions while appearing to be sane. In light of Beverly's and my separate, but mutually stifling, Lutheran upbringings, along with the accompanying puritan guilt and attitude, we both managed to share and together explore ideas of sex that few couples risk engaging in. The fact that my wife would share personal photos of her nude body to strangers, and I facilitate this public display, we have breached a morality that to us for years felt strangling and altogether untrue. Desire that remains in hiding behind polite and superficial masks of sanity prohibits a truly honest discourse. But I grant you, our love for each other has always been anchored in an historically incendiary relationship which still habitually excites me especially, confounding and disrupting conventional norms of society. Taking photos of my naked girl out and about on the many trails in the Huron National Forest, or on a secluded beach at Tawas Point, as well as numerous early morning gonzo activities along several streets in downtown Louisville and sleepy Apalachicola, afforded stimulating pleasures as well as images we now cherish as our vitality continues to wane. And as we look back on these collaborations we are neither embarrassed nor afraid of any judgmental consequences. Erotic fantasies are parcels of our life together, and *things in themselves* we willingly made. Our efforts were obsessively patterned to make up for lost time, to somehow add balance to the twelve years missing in our relationship from the age of seventeen to twenty-nine. And as she was turning forty my boldest request ever came when I asked her to take off her clothes for me and reveal through my photography her magnificence. It took enormous courage for her to allow me this liberty. Beverly Lane has always been amazing, and even though I will eternally resent her for not initially throwing in with me way back when, I am grateful for the many years we eventually had together. Regrets today mostly center on the quickening prospect of our running out of time.

About the Author

M Sarki maintains a most curious literary blog at https://msarki.tumblr.com where he publishes his critical views on many subjects, including books read, as well as a periodic attempt at creating artifact. Since 2000 M Sarki has published four collections of poetry and three books of prose. He has written, directed, and produced four short art films titled *Gnoman's Bois de Rose, Biscuits and Striola, The Tools of Migrant Hunters, My Father's Kitchen,* and is the exclusive author of the feature film screenplay, *Alphonso Bow*.